The
Religious
Life
Defined

THE RELIGIOUS LIFE DEFINED

*an official commentary on
the deliberations of
the Second Vatican Council*

edited by
Rev. Ralph M. Wiltgen, S.V.D.
Divine Word Missionary

Divine Word Publications
Techny, Illinois

Grateful acknowledgement is extended to
Guild Press for use of quoted material from
The Documents of Vatican II edited by W.
M. Abbott, S.J. Copyright © 1966.

Library of Congress Catalog Card Number: 79-134495

Standard Book Number: 87298-121-5

Divine Word Publications is an apostolate of
the Society of the Divine Word serving the
people of God throughout the world by
spreading the Word.

Printed in the United States of America

Dedicated to
the World's Two Million Religious

Contents

Chapter One

INTRODUCTION

Chapter One

INTRODUCTION

This book is for the most part a translation of an Official Commentary on the chapter about Religious in the Dogmatic Constitution on the Church.

Whenever comment by the author is made in subsequent chapters, this is always clearly indicated, and is explained in the final paragraph of this chapter.

The Official Commentary here presented in translation was prepared by the Doctrinal Commission of Vatican II. Besides indicating all the amendments and qualifications presented by the council fathers on the second and third drafts of the chapter on Religious, it also contains the detailed observations and decisions made by the Doctrinal Commission regarding these drafts. In each case the Official Commentary points out why certain amendments and qualifications were accepted and why others were rejected.

In its printed Latin form the Official Commentary covers 33 pages in various booklets (8 x 11½ inches). The booklets were distributed to the council fathers for private study prior to their voting on the acceptability of the third and fourth drafts of the chapter on Religious.

The first draft along with the balance of the schema on the Church had been sent back to the Doctrinal Commission for revision without being discussed. The second draft was thoroughly discussed in the council hall and amended through oral and written proposals, but was not voted upon. When the third draft — that is, the former second draft now in amended form — was voted on, the council fathers were free to submit qualifications with their affirmative votes (in Latin: *placet iuxta modum*). The fourth draft — the former third one now corrected by some qualifications — became the final draft.

Just as during Vatican II this Official Commentary was indispensable for the council fathers in acquiring a proper understanding of the text on which they were voting, so too today the Official Commentary is indispensable for anyone who wishes to know the full and real meaning of the teaching contained in the fourth and final draft of the chapter on Religious in the Dogmatic Constitution on the Church.

Technical Aspects

This commentary would be quite unintelligible if one did not have at hand the text of the chapter on Religious. Since *The Documents of Vatican II by* Abbott-Gallagher are so widely diffused throughout the English-speaking world, and since the British edition is a copy of the American one page for page and line for line, the author will use this translation as a basic reference and refer to it simply as Abbott-Gallagher.[1] Errors or inaccuracies in this translation will become apparent or will be pointed out as the commentary proceeds. How such errors or inaccuracies crept into the translation is explained by Abbott-Gallagher on page ix.

---

[1] **The Documents of Vatican II: All Sixteen Official Texts Promulgated by the Ecumenical Council 1963-1965,** Translated from the Latin; Walter M. Abbott, S.J., General Editor; Very Rev. Msgr. Joseph Gallagher, Translation Editor (New York: Guild Press, America Press, Association Press, 1966), xxii and 793 pp. Also, **ibid.** (Geoffrey Chapman: London, Dublin, Melbourne, 1967).

"As a general rule," the authors say on page x, "the translations in this volume start a new paragraph wherever the original does, but they often start one where the original does not."

Since the Official Commentary of the Doctrinal Commission referred to the paragraphing as it was in Latin, some adjusting of Abbott-Gallagher to the Official Commentary is necessary. This can be done by assigning the same lettering to the passages in Abbott-Gallagher as is used in the Official Commentary. The reader simply places capital letters in the margins of his copy of Abbott-Gallagher and indicates with lines or brackets the extent of each passage, thus:

Number 43, pages 73-74: A—first paragraph
                                    B—second and third paragraphs
                                    C-fourth or last paragraph
Number 44, pages 74-75: A—first line
                                    B—first and second paragraphs
                                    C—third paragraph
                                    D—fourth and fifth paragraphs
                                    E—sixth or last paragraph
Number 45, pages 75-77: A—first two paragraphs
                                    B—third paragraph
                                    C—fourth or last paragraph
Number 46, pages 77-78: A—first line
                                    B—first paragraph
                                    C—second paragraph
                                    D—third paragraph
                                    E—fourth or last paragraph
Number 47, page 78:   A—first line
                                    B—the paragraph

Historical Background

During the preliminary phase of Vatican II the preparatory commission on Religious requested the preparatory Doctrinal Commission to include in its schema on the Church something about religious orders because they constituted "an integral part of the Church." Consequently the fifth of the eleven chapters in the first draft of the schema on the Church was titled, *The States of Life Devoted to Acquiring Evangelical Perfection*. The Doctrinal Commission requested and received authorization from Pope John XXIII on November 10, 1962 — a month after the council had opened — to distribute this schema to the council fathers.[2]

The chapter on the Religious life covered three pages and consisted of:

Number 17	The Evangelical Counsels
Number 18	The Importance of the State of Perfection in the Church
Number 19	The Position Occupied by the States of Perfection in the Church

In addition there was half a page of footnotes.

According to a notice on the first page of the schema or draft text, the titles of the individual numbers were to be dropped in the final draft. They were meant to serve merely as a very brief indication of the contents of the number, and if joined together could provide an outline.

For numerous reasons — overlapping, for one — the schema on the Church along with five others was completely reorganized by the Doctrinal Commission of the council. In an effort to expedite this work the council's coordinating commission (made up of 7 Cardinals) created a joint commission made up of members from both

---

[2] Schemata Constitutionum et Decretorum de quibus disceptabitur in Concilii sessionibus, Series Secunda: De Ecclesia et de B. Maria Virgine (Polyglot Press, Vatican City, 1962), 123 pp.

the Doctrinal Commission and the commission on Religious to review the chapter on the Religious life. At its meetings in 1963, between the first and second sessions of the council, the joint commission agreed upon a new title for this chapter, namely, *Those Who Profess the Evangelical Counsels.*

But when the schema on the Church was issued in revised form by the Doctrinal Commission later in 1963 it was made up of these four chapters:

I.   The Mystery of the Church
II.   The Hierarchic Constitution of the Church
III. The People of God with Special Reference to the Laity
IV. The Call to Holiness in the Church

The fourth and final chapter had absorbed the chapter on Religious life. It covered 5½ pages and contained Numbers 28 to 36 as follows:

Number 28   Introduction
Number 29   The Universal Call to Holiness
Number 30   Holiness Which Is One Is Practiced in Many Forms
Number 31   Means for Acquiring Holiness, and the Evangelical Counsels
Number 32   The Practice of the Counsels in a State of Life Sanctioned by the Church
Number 33   The Importance in the Church of the States Devoted to Acquiring Perfection
Number 34   Under the Authority of the Church

An accompanying booklet contained 25 amendments to chapter IV presented in writing by two groups of council fathers and by three individual council fathers. These amendments gave no indication why the Doctrinal Commission had decided not to accept the proposal of the joint commission, nor why instead it had created a new chapter which absorbed the chapter on Religious life.

At the last minute, just before chapter III and chapter IV were to be printed in a booklet for distribution to the council fathers, the coordinating commission of the council decided that chapter III ought to be divided into two parts. The first part was to be called *The People of God in General,* and would form chapter II of the Constitution on the Church, and the other part was to be called *The Laity in Particular,* and would form chapter IV.

And so instead of having four chapters, as printed in the text, the Constitution would ultimately have these five chapters as indicated in a first-page footnote:

I.   The Mystery of the Church
II.   The People of God in General
III.   The Hierarchic Constitution of the Church
IV.   The Laity in Particular
V.   The Call to Holiness in the Church

[3] Schemata Constitutionum et Decretorum de quibus disceptabitur in Concilii sessionibus: Schema Constitutionis Dogmaticae De Ecclesia (Polyglot Press, Vatican City, 1963), Pars I, 47 pp; Pars II, 31 pp.

This decision of the coordinating commission did not at all affect the previous chapter IV, which now simply became chapter V.[4]

Wondering what had happened to the chapter on Religious life between the first and second sessions, the council fathers who were Superiors General called a meeting in Rome on October 14, 1963, two weeks after the second session began. They were given the above historical background by Bishop Henry Compagnone, a Discalced Carmelite, who was a member of the commission on Religious and had also been a member of the preparatory commission on Religious.

He told the Superiors General that the commission on Religious was not altogether pleased with the revisions made by the Doctrinal Commission. His commission, he said, liked very much the new emphasis on the teaching that all members of the Church are called to holiness, but was displeased with what he called a defective presentation of the nature of Religious life. His commission was also of the view, he added, that all statements on the universal call to holiness should be transferred to the chapter on *The People of God in General,* and that chapter V instead should be titled simply, *Religious.* All other chapters could remain as they were.

As a result of this meeting, the Superiors General decided to give their support to the proposal of the commission on Religious. Individual Superiors General were of course free to take another stand if they wished, but nearly all of them gave their support to the proposals of the commission on Religious. Chapter V was discussed in

---

[4] Cf. **Emendationes a Concilii Patribus scripto exhibitae super schema Constitutionis dogmaticae De Ecclesia, Pars II** (Polyglot Press, Vatican City, 1963), pp. 17-19

the council on October 25, 29, 30 and 31, and the ideas of the commission on Religious were repeatedly mentioned in the speeches of the 48 council fathers who took the floor.

Earlier some council fathers had suggested that the schema on the Blessed Virgin Mary should not become a separate council document, but rather that it should be incorporated as chapter VI in the schema on the Church. And so on October 29, while chapter V on *The Call to Holiness in the Church* was being discussed, a vote was taken to see if it was "agreeable to the fathers that the schema on the Blessed Virgin Mary, Mother of the Church, be adapted in order to constitute chapter VI of the schema on the Church." The required majority of votes was 1097. The results were:

Yes	1114
No	1074
Void	5
Total	2193

So now the schema on the Church had a sixth chapter on the Blessed Virgin Mary.

Some council fathers who were both bishops and members of religious orders were convinced — after the discussion of chapter V — that the Cardinal moderators had unjustly refused them the opportunity of speaking their minds on the council floor and swiftly took action. On their initiative The Bishops Secretariat was founded on November 11. The first of the 7 presidents elected by the 42 bishops, from as many different religious orders, present on this occasion, was Archbishop Pacifico Perantoni, a former Superior General of the Franciscans. The Bishops Secretariat set up its headquarters in the Jesuit Generalate just two blocks away from St. Peter's

Basilica where the council was being held; but used only the street address: Borgo Santo Spirito 5.

The vast majority of Superiors General immediately joined forces with The Bishops Secretariat because they had not been very successful alone. Intense activity followed. In two weeks' time the united efforts of the Superiors General and The Bishops Secretariat won support from 679 council fathers — including 17 Cardinals — for certain specific amendments to the schema on the Church. These amendments and the list of corresponding signatures reached Pope Paul VI who passed them on with a personal note to the Doctrinal Commission "for diligent and careful study."

The Doctrinal Commission then took these specific amendments into consideration when it amended the second draft of the schema on the Church. And on July 3, 1964, between the second and third sessions, the Doctrinal Commission received authorization from Pope Paul VI to distribute its 219-page revision of the schema on the Church to the council fathers. This book contained the *Textus prior* (second draft) and the *Textus emendatus* (third draft) in parallel columns, so that the council fathers could see at a glance what alterations had been made. The changes were printed in italics. (See Appendix, Chapter Ten)

From this point onwards the record can be taken directly from the official reports on the texts in question prepared by the Doctrinal Commission for the council fathers.

> **NOTE: In the pages which follow, paragraphs like this which appear inset and in bold face are comment by the author and are so designated.**

All else is translated from the official Latin reports of the Doctrinal Commission (including italics). The purpose of the author's comment is clarification. Information in brackets has also been added by the author.[5]

[5] For more details on the historical background, cf. Ralph M. Wiltgen, S.V.D., **The Rhine Flows into the Tiber:** The Unknown Council (Hawthorn Books, New York, 1967) pp. 103-109. For the ballot returns on the Blessed Virgin Mary chapter, see: Giovanni Caprile, S.J., **Il Concilio Vaticano II:** Secondo Periodo 1963-1964, Vol III (Edizioni "La Civiltà Cattolica," Roma 1966) pp. 160-163.

Chapter Two

THE GENERAL REPORT

Chapter Two

THE GENERAL REPORT[6]

This general report refers to that material of the Constitution on the Church which in the present schema follows the chapter on "The Laity," and which deals both with "the call of all to holiness" and with "Religious." This material corresponds to the undivided chapter IV of the previous schema which was titled simply, "The Universal Call to Holiness in the Church." Before reporting on other items it seems opportune to inform the fathers of the reason for the present revision and the manner in which it was carried out.

Reason for the Revision

Many observations were presented orally and in writing by fathers on chapter IV of the previous schema, filling more than 500 pages. Worthy of mention among them is the proposal made by the Most Eminent Doepfner and 74 fathers, and in particular the schema introduced by the Most Reverend Butler and the fathers of the Order of St. Benedict. In addition our Doctrinal Commission also received certain observations on this same chapter IV signed by 679 fathers, which had to be given immediate and very close attention and consideration when the task of revision was begun.

At first the Doctrinal Commission designated a sub-

---

[6] Schema Constitutionis De Ecclesia (Polyglot Press, Vatican City, 1964), pp. 167-173.

commission of five fathers from its own members to make this revision in accord with the wishes of all the fathers. In the course of this subcommission's work—starting with the fourth meeting held on January 28, 1964—five more fathers were added from the council's commission on Religious. The result was, in fact, a joint subcommission made up of the following fathers from the Doctrinal Commission: Browne, Charue, Seper, Gut, Butler, Fernandez. From the commission on Religious were: Compagnone, Sipovic, Stein, Kleiner, Sepinski. The Most Eminent Browne and the Most Reverend Sepinski were able to be present for only one meeting. The others, however, were usually always present.

The subcommission had the following *periti:* Abellan, Benjamin of the Most Holy Trinity, Boyer, Gambari, Gagnebet, Labourdette, Lio—who was also entrusted with the office of secretary and relator – Philipon, Rahner, Tascon, Thils, and Verardo. Present at some of the meetings were also the secretaries general of the Doctrinal Commission and the commission on Religious. Most of the *periti* were always at the service of the fathers. Eleven meetings were held to revise the text. And at the very end, when the new revision was finally proposed, the president in his concluding remarks was able to give thanks to all "for the tranquil, harmonious, and fruitful labor of this subcommission," as one can read in the minutes.

The purpose of the joint subcommission's work was to weigh the whole matter once again—both what pertained to the universal call to holiness and what referred to Religious. For this reason their first task was to obtain a synthesized view of all the wishes of the fathers. This was accomplished by having the *periti* draw up three reports.

The first one (drawn up by Father Lio) dealt with observations and questions of a general nature proposed by the fathers.

The second one (drawn up by Father Thils) contained specific observations dealing with the universal call to holiness.

The third one (drawn up by Father Philipon) presented questions and observations which specifically referred to Religious.

The method of procedure was as follows: Since there were innumerable observations of a specific nature, some which were not rarely discordant with others, preference was given to those which were more important and more fundamental. At times, however, a middle course was used in order to reconcile diverse views, insofar as this was possible and as long as the purity, integrity and security of the doctrine were maintained. For this reason those very fathers from the commission on Religious were of the greatest assistance in preventing further difficulties. By their help the new revision was approved by unanimous vote of the joint subcommission.

After the subcommission had completed its work, the text was presented in a plenary session of the Doctrinal Commission together with the above-mentioned reports and another which dealt specifically with the amendments (drawn up by the same *peritus* who was relator). Here, after being examined anew and when some amendments were made, the text likewise received unanimous approval. Left pending, however, was the question of how to arrange the material. This question, which is still pending, will be discussed below.

Preliminary Questions

Certain preliminary questions resulted from the wishes of the fathers and had to be given careful consideration.

Considered first were the judgments made by the fathers in a general way on the material taken as a whole. A synthesis of all these general judgments was presented in the first report. At this point it is well to mention briefly that many fathers approved of the material in general, except for certain points. The majority, however, (of which the 679 signing fathers were a part) pointed out serious difficulties regarding both the arrangement of the material and the doctrine itself. It is difficult to give the exact numbers of fathers, however the ensemble of considerations showed that to all appearances a notable divergence separated the fathers, even with regard to the general judgments.

On the other hand consideration had to be given to the fact that the fathers had already approved the text of the entire Constitution on the Church in general, making it the basis of discussion and capable of further improvement. Besides this, many fathers (actually the majority) said nothing and wrote nothing. In light of all these considerations a middle way was used for the new revision. It was decided not to reject everything that came from the previous text nor to retain all of it, and not to present it to the fathers once again completely unchanged nor to revise everything anew. The previous text was retained where this proved suitable; amendments were made and integral parts were added. At times these latter were neither of slight nor of minor importance, as is clear from the report on the amendments itself.

Another rather noteworthy question in the observations made by the fathers was the following: Should chapter IV of the previous schema remain as it was as far as arrangement of the material was concerned? Or should it rather be divided, with the first numbers (on the universal call) being transferred to another place in the Constitution on the Church, so that there would be a distinct chapter devoted entirely to Religious? The reasons presented were seriously pondered, although at times they were quite contradictory. In general not a few fathers explicitly or implicitly approved for various reasons the arrangement of the material as it was, namely, joined together. Some of these defended their thesis in the name of others.

But on the other hand many fathers, (like the 679 mentioned at the beginning), explicitly and formally requested that there be a chapter reserved for Religious, and that the material on the universal call to holiness be transferred to the chapter on the People of God. This caused a difficulty for the subcommission. The evolution of this matter as contained in the minutes was as follows: After a long discussion on this question in the joint subcommission, during which nearly all eleven fathers and nearly all twelve *periti* spoke, the Most Eminent Cardinal Browne, then holding the office of president, presented the conclusions. He asserted that all finally were in agreement on these points:

First, that at least something should be said about universal holiness in the chapter on the People of God; this would be by way of announcing a further and more extensive treatment in another place.

And secondly, that the part which refers to the universal call to holiness ought to be treated separately from the part which refers to Religious.

The fathers, however, did not reach agreement on the third point, namely: Whether there should be two *chapters,* one of which was to be reserved exclusively for Religious, or whether there should not rather be one chapter with two *sections,* one of which was to be reserved for Religious. The Most Eminent President therefore asked the fathers to vote, and the outcome was as follows: 4 fathers (namely, Charue, Seper, Stein, Butler) were in favor of *one* chapter with two *sections;* the first section would treat of the vocation of all men to holiness and the second would treat of Religious. 7 fathers (namely, Browne, Compagnone, Sipovic, Gut, Kleiner, Fernandez, Sepinski) voted for two *chapters*, one of which was to be reserved for Religious.

As is clear from the minutes the same question was also referred to a small subcommission (Charue, Garrone, Florit) of the Doctrinal Commission. Although this subcommission of itself preferred two *sections,* it nevertheless left the decision to the plenary Doctrinal Commission. It is a fact that after the text was approved at the plenary session of the Doctrinal Commission held in March, 1964, the above question was supposed to be decided as well. But either because there was not enough time, or – as the Most Eminent President indicated – because some had asked that this question should rather be decided in a plenary joint session since the matter had been examined in the first place in a joint subcommission, the solution was postponed by the Most Eminent President until the meetings to be held in the coming month of June. But during June the matter was not decided because at that time no plenary meeting of the joint commission was held.

As regards the question of the title, it was agreed unanimously that in any case the part reserved to those who profess religious vows was to be entitled simply: "Religious."

On the Universal
Call to Holiness

Here it is apropos to explain something about the views of the fathers concerning that part of the text which treats of the universal call to holiness. The more important points are these:

1. Nearly all of the fathers approved of retaining in the schema the principle of the universal call to holiness. Therefore in revising the text this part has been retained, although it refers more to the moral order than to the order of being and of constituting the Church. Provision existed, however, for adding certain things in the *preface* concerning the holiness of the Church itself from an ontological and fundamental point of view.

> **COMMENT: Cf. Abbott-Gallagher, pages 65-66, Number 39, first 8 lines. The Doctrinal Commission revised this passage to state that the Church itself is holy, and that Christ, who alone is holy, willed to have the Church be holy and made it so. The purpose of the Church's holiness is also indicated: for God's glory.[7]**

2. Very many fathers (especially the 679 noted) asked that after affirming the unity in holiness it should also be taught that there is diversity in holiness according to various degrees. Therefore in the new text the

[7] Ibid., p. 147

affirmation of *one* holiness remains and the addition is not made as was done in the previous text, that holiness is also *the same.* Thus the new text recognizes implicitly that there is diversity according to various degrees and vocations. And further, in the whole section now reserved for Religious, the religious vocation itself is presented in a more distinct and more particularized way in the new revision, because of the description contained in Number 44 on the nature and importance of the religious state in the Church.

> **COMMENT: The first sentence in Number 41 of Abbott-Gallagher, page 67, is incorrect. It reads: "In the various types and duties of life, one and the same holiness is cultivated by all who are moved by the Spirit of God . . ." The words "and the same" are not in the text as approved by the Vatican Council, for the reasons given above. (In Latin:** *In variis vitae generibus et officiis una sanctitas excolitur ab omnibus, qui a Spiritu Dei aguntur . . .)*

3. Many fathers (nearly 200) asked to have the notion and nature of holiness included. This request was satisfied, not by giving some scholastic description of holiness, but by adding various elements here and there, especially by introducing texts from sacred scripture. In this way a clear picture is given of the very nature of holiness under the aspect of its essence, under its dynamic aspect, and under the aspect of the ways and means by which it is acquired.

4. Not a few Fathers (about 100) wanted something said about the nature of charity in relation to holiness; or they asked that express mention be made of faith and hope; or they wished that all other precepts and virtues

as well should be inculcated. Charity is mentioned twice in the new draft, although not of course in the manner of a theological dissertation. In addition, faith and hope are also mentioned.

Thus the new draft explicitly says in Number 41: "Certainly everyone ought to advance unhesitatingly according to his own gifts and duties along the path of a *living faith,* which arouses *hope* and which acts *through charity."* In this way the total force of the theological virtues in the practice of holiness is stated explicitly, as the fathers wished.

> **COMMENT:** The sentence as translated in the first paragraph of Number 41 in Abbott-Gallagher, page 68, seems less clear.

As to the other precepts and virtues, the text of Number 42 already states by way of a general principle that every member of the faithful must also "apply himself constantly . . . to the practice *of all virtues,* in order that . . . charity may grow like a good seed in his soul and bring forth fruit." The excess of separating charity from the practice of all other virtues is thus avoided.

Virtue necessarily has correlates, namely, precepts and counsels. Here and there, then, the following particular moral virtues are expressly mentioned: mercy, benignity, humility, modesty, patience, fortitude, justice, chastity, poverty, obedience, abnegation. Consequently one can draw from this the implicit conclusion that charity itself and also holiness require that all commandments be observed, as 1 John 5, 3, admonishes: "For this is the love of God (in Latin: "Haec est enim *charitas* Dei . . ."), that we keep his commandments" (cf. also John 14, 21; 2 John 6).

In section Number 42, paragraph 3 (in Abbott-Gallagher it is paragraph 5) it is expressly stated that the evangelical counsels assist everyone in acquiring the perfection of charity, no matter what his particular state might be. And thus the prejudice is avoided that might look upon perfection itself and also holiness as if they were the monopoly of those who are Religious.

5. Some fathers expressly requested that emphasis should be placed upon the imitation of Christ, the Blessed Virgin Mary, and the saints, as a means for acquiring holiness. As for other means, they said that the Most Holy Eucharist certainly ought to be indicated explicitly. The reply to these requests is that at the very beginning of Number 40, Christ is called "the divine Teacher and *Model* of all perfection." And as the text progresses there is mention more than once of the imitation and following of Christ.

The Most Holy Eucharist is expressly mentioned among other means in the new revision. Mention is also made of the history of the saints (at the very end of Number 40), and for priests, the emulation of good priests is expressly recommended. As regards the Blessed Virgin Mary, this is mentioned later in a separate chapter of the Constitution on the Church.

> COMMENT: In Number 65 in the Chapter on the Blessed Virgin Mary (Abbott-Gallagher, page 93, first paragraph) the text reads: ". . . the followers of Christ . . . raise their eyes to Mary who shines forth to the whole community of the elect as a model of the virtues. Devotedly meditating on her and contemplating her . . . the Church . . . becomes ever increasingly like her Spouse."

6. A great many Fathers requested that not only should there be treatment of the holiness of the Church

in general, along with some mention of the miseries of its members, but that the text should treat also of that holiness toward which the various members of the Church (bishops, priests, ministers, husbands and wives, workers, etc.) must strive. The text at the same time, they said, ought to keep in mind the particular aspects of the profession that one follows.

All of these requests have been satisfied in the newly revised Number 41. Of the sins of those who are also members of the Church it is simply stated (Number 40): "Since we all truly offend in many things (cf. James 3, 2), we all need God's mercy continuously and must daily pray: 'and forgive us our debts' " (Matt. 6, 12).

7. According to the wishes of the fathers care was taken in the new revision so that not only the text, "For this is the will of God, your sanctification," has been enunciated as a fundamental principle (cf. Introduction), but also express mention has been made here and there of the necessity of our conformity to the divine will for acquiring holiness. For the new draft reads (Number 41, last paragraph): "and if they cooperate with the *divine* will;" and again (Number 42, paragraph 1): "And with the help of His grace fulfill His *will* by deeds."

> **COMMENT**: **At this time the provisional title of Number 39 (formerly Number 28) was** *Introduction.* **The text referred to is quoted there. Cf. Abbott-Gallagher, pages 65-66, Number 39, first paragraph.**

The inner nature of Christian holiness itself, however, shines forth here and there in the entire text and context (cf. e.g. Number 40). Thus it is affirmed (Number 40, paragraph 2) that the faithful actually are not only called by God to holiness, but also "in fact have been made holy," and that for this reason they ought to cling to that holiness and grow in it. And so it is apparent that holiness in the Church is not merely an ideal and something static, but rather a certain true reality that is mystical and dynamic, one that continues on and that grows within the souls of men with the help of Christ's grace.

On Religious

1. As was mentioned, the evangelical counsels have already been treated in the section on the universal call to holiness. In the same place, according to the wishes of the fathers, express mention has been made of the value and importance for all of martyrdom (Number 42, paragraph 2), of the state of virginity dedicated to God (*ibid.,* paragraph 3), and also of course of the value and importance of poverty and obedience in imitation of Christ (*ibid.,* paragraph 4). The state of virginity dedicated to God is here said to be held "in particular honor by the Church" (so as to fulfill as well the wish of the 679 fathers).

> **COMMENT**: Paragraphs 2, 3 and 4 in the Latin text are respectively paragraphs 3, 5 and 6 in Abbott-Gallagher, Number 42, pages 71-72.

At the very beginning of Number 43, however, where the text begins to speak only of Religious, the divine origin is affirmed for those counsels which are professed by Religious in a particular way on the basis of a pact firmly sealed by vows. This was done to make immediately evident not only the divine origin of the counsels, as those 679 fathers had requested, but also to make immediately evident the ultimate link whereby – under the authority of the Church – the religious state goes back to a divine origin. For the evangelical counsels themselves, as is said in the schema, "are a divine gift which the Church has received from her Lord and which she ever preserves by His grace. It is also her responsibility to regulate their *practice* and to devise as well *stable* forms of living according to them" (Number 43). Thus the very origin and also the evolution of the religious state in the Church are placed in their proper light.

> **COMMENT**: The logic here is that the religious state has a divine origin in so far as the evangelical counsels which it professes come from Christ. But since the evangelical counsels have been given by Christ to His Church as a gift, and not to individuals or groups, and since it is the Church that preserves the counsels with the help of Christ's grace, it follows that the religious state must need be under the authority of the Church. The link connecting the religious state with a divine origin, in other words, passes through the Church. In connection with the portion of Number 43 quoted here, see Qualification 11, page 77, this book.

2. Also in the new draft at the beginning of Number 44 the essential *nature* of the religious state is described. It is one thing to observe the evangelical counsels as counsels, as all others can do, and quite another thing — something substantially different — to oblige oneself to observe these counsels by *vows*. For through these perpetual vows, taken in a state sanctioned by the Church, a member of the faithful is committed "in his person and with all that he has to the service of God, and to His honor, by a new and special title." In fact, as is expressly stated, "a person gives himself over *totally* to God whom he loves above all else."

Here it seems the request of so many fathers (also the 679), which asked that this perpetual, total and indivisible *consecration* of Religious to God be stressed, has been satisfied. From what follows, however, it is apparent that the pre-eminence of the state of those who are Religious also springs from this principle, because in the text it is said explicitly that a Religious "by these same vows is *more intimately* consecrated to divine service." In this way the essentially theological and theocentric aspect of the religious life is asserted.

> **COMMENT: See Qualification 20, page 81, for the reason why "by these same vows" was changed to read: "by profession of the evangelical counsels in the Church."**

3. *The Christlike aspect* of the religious state is made manifest in various places. But it is especially clear in Number 46. Here again the observations made by very many fathers have been provided for.

4. *The ecclesial aspect* of the religious state is shown first in Number 43, but more space is devoted to it in Numbers 44 and 45. As desired by many fathers (among them the 679), care was taken here lest the total ecclesial aspect be thought of in terms of an exterior apostolate. Therefore it is here most particularly stated that Religious participate in the mystery of the Church through the *charity* toward which the evangelical counsels lead them. And this occurs, of course (as has been added in Number 44, paragraph 2), "in keeping with the form of their particular vocation," either *"through prayer* or through active undertakings as well." In fact in the same place, at the end, it has been added that "the Church preserves and fosters the *particular* characteris-

tics of the various institutes of Religious." All of this explains and makes clear the meaning of the ecclesial aspect and the meaning of the contemplative life (about which there is also something in Number 46, paragraph 1), which is highly esteemed.

> **COMMENT: Paragraph 2 of Number 44, mentioned above, is paragraph 3 in Abbott-Gallagher, pages 74-75. The Abbott-Gallagher translation here says incompletely: "The chosen means may be prayer or active undertakings." This is disjunctive. The Latin says that Religious have the duty of exerting themselves for the Kingdom of Christ "through prayer or through active undertakings as well" (in Latin: *sive oratione, sive actuosa quoque opera*). This is not disjunctive, but explicitly includes prayer in either case.**

5. *The aspect of sign and of testimony,* which some fathers urgently requested, has been retained; but it is contained in Number 44 in a completely revised form. Now there no longer occur, among other things, these words of the former draft: "in the *first place* it has the value of a sign," which the 679 fathers lamented. The life of Religious by its nature ought to testify to all, that it is possible to observe each precept by the grace of God and by deference toward God. If there are Religious who in fact oblige themselves for their entire lives, and under vows as well, to observe the counsels — which thus are transformed for them into precepts — it then becomes all the more evident that the precepts common to all men are not beyond the strength of a single man assisted by grace.

6. *Also the eschatological aspect* of the religious state can be seen in the new draft, in Number 44, according to

the wishes of the fathers. This is something really necessary, especially in our times when men are somewhat preoccupied with the goods of this world, and not with eternal life and the glory of the heavenly kingdom. The religious state of itself serves as a witness to this life and glory and gives advance knowledge of them to the world.

7. Other proposals of the fathers concerning points such as the authority of the Church are now to be found in Number 45 where the text of the previous draft has been revised and expanded. (Some of these points were, for example, the need to give a theological basis for the exemption of Religious being a right of the Pontiff who is Primate; also, ideas with regard to liturgical acts of the Church and the religious state.)

8. A revision has also been made of the previous text of Number 46 (formerly Number 35) according to various suggestions made by the fathers.

Now that this *Report* is finished, we give our most sincere thanks to all the fathers with the hope that it will contribute to the glory and increase of universal holiness and of religious life in the Church of Christ.

Chapter Three

REPORT BY
PARAGRAPH NUMBER

Chapter Three

REPORT BY PARAGRAPH NUMBER[8]

**Report on
Number 43**

Provisional title: **On the Profession of the Evangelical Counsels in the Church**

The Chapter or distinct section reserved for Religious
begins with this Number.

> **COMMENT: The capital letters in paren-
> theses at the beginning of each of the follow-
> ing sections are explained above in Chapter 1
> under the subdivision "Technical Aspects."
> (See also the NOTE on page 115 in this work.)**

(A) The first passage, "The evangelical counsels . . .
according to them," lays down the fundamental principle of the *divine origin* of the evangelical *counsels.*
Intentionally and by his grace Christ donated and preserves these counsels in his Church so that they might be
observed and regulated, subject to the magisterium and
authority of the Church itself, also through the introduction of stabilized forms. This assertion fulfills the wish
of the 679 fathers who requested that the divine origin
should be affirmed for those evangelical counsels that
are to be observed by Religious in a state of life sanctioned by the Church. The expression "state of acquiring
perfection" is not used; nor is this technical expression
used either by the Commission for Religious. Cf.

---

[8] **Ibid.,** pp. 161-166.

E/1145, 1289, 1465. Nor was it desired to propose what might strictly speaking be called a "definition" of a Religious.

> **COMMENT: The numbers (E/1145, 1289, 1465) in the second to last sentence are a file reference, for the currently inaccessible archives of Vatican II. Such file references contain no names, but merely indicate the folders containing the proposals made in signed documents by council fathers.**

(B) The second passage, "Thus it has . . . road of charity," is intimately connected with the preceding one. *The fact* is asserted that there truly are various forms of life followed by those who are Religious, which have sprung up in the Church from that root given to the Church by God. The first and second passages include certain things found in the previous draft. Mention is made of the *solitary life* which flourished extensively in the Church, especially in the first centuries. Then follows an enumeration of the *chief benefits* which flow from the nature of religious life; cf. v.g. E/1196, 1258.

As for *primitive monasticism,* desired by E/1168, and the *contemplative* life mentioned by E/1274, note the following: The ascetics, the anchorites, the continent, the virgins, and the widows of the distant past made a profession of the evangelical counsels without establishing what could properly speaking be called an Institute. They remained, however, under the vigilance and protection of the Church. Documentation is provided by these authors: R. Draguet, *Les Peres du Desert,* Paris 1949; P. De Meester, "De monachico statu iuxta disciplinam byzantinam," Rome 1942, pp. 70-76 and 312 ff. (Cf. *ibid.* p. 70 ff.) "Hesychasta est qui solus soli adloquitur Deo et continuo Eum exorat." Clement of Alexandria, *Stromata,* III, 1: PG 8, 110 AB. Origines, *In Ier.,* Homily 19, 7: PG 13, 517. St. Cyprian, *Hab. Virg.* 4: PL 4, 455 ff.

NOTE: A text from Pius XII's Allocution *Nous sommes heureux,* 11 April 1958, AAS 50 (1958) was cited in the previous draft of this schema (1963) in footnote 14, page 27.

(C) The third passage or paragraph 2, "From the point . . . mission of the Church," takes up once more the text of the previous draft, with some additions and with some changes. *Hierarchical* is added at the beginning of the passage, so that the specific aspect may be better determined. And at the end this addition has been made: *"and so that they all in their own way can forward the saving mission of the Church,"* in order that the importance of the religious state for the life and mission of the Church in the world might be evident right from the beginning. Both laity and clergy alike can be affiliated with Secular Institutes, as Pius XII declared in *Provida Mater* (see p. 61). The text, however, does not enter into juridical or controverted questions.

> COMMENT: The Abbott-Gallagher translation speaks here of "the divine and hierarchical *structure* of the Church." And at the end of Number 44 it speaks again of "the hierarchical *structure* of the Church." In the latter case the Latin text does have "structure" (i.e. *structura*), but in the former case the Latin has "constitution" (i.e. *constitutio*). "Structure" is only one ele-

ment in the divine constitution of the Church.

**Report on
Number 44**

Provisional title: **On the Nature and Importance of the Religious State in the Church.**

(A) After the Commission had discussed the matter in a plenary session, it was decided not to invert the sequence of Numbers 44 and 45, but to retain the sequence that existed before. As one can see, the title for this Number has been changed from the previous draft, to show that here particular treatment is given to the *nature* of the religious state. And from its nature is derived its consequent *importance.* And in order to avoid the difficulties which many had foreseen, the expression "religious state" is used in the title in place of "the state of acquiring perfection." This too corresponds with the wish expressed by the entire subcommission, namely, that one speak simply of "Religious" or of "the religious state."

(B) The first passage or paragraph 1, "The faithful... His Spouse, the Church," is *new* with respect to the previous draft and has been added so that the inherent nature of the religious state at once becomes evident as a relationship to God and a consecration through vows. Cf. E/1326, 1220, 1228, 1236, 1258, 1380. For it is evident that the *state* of a Religious differs from that of another precisely and primarily because of the fact that the Religious *obliges himself,* by vows, to observe the evangelical counsels. These counsels then transform the Religious into a person *totally given over to God.* For St. Thomas writes in chapter 15 of *De perfectione vitae spiritualis,* "If then (someone) has placed his entire life under obligation to God by vow, promising to serve him with works of perfection, such a one has already simply assumed for himself the condition or state of perfection." In this way an answer is provided for many fathers who requested that more express and more precise mention should be made of the nature of the religious state and its consecration.

Many stressed this *theocentric* aspect emphatically. It is evident that the *perpetual* bond is the principal one. A temporary bond is often assumed by way of probation, with the intention of making a perpetual dedication, under the supposition that there is a vocation from God. The sacrifice is not total for those who have only temporary vows, because "holocaust means that someone offers to God the whole of what he has," as St. Thomas says in: *Summa Theol.* II-II, q. 186, a. 7. For an earlier text see: St. Gregory the Great, *In Ezech.* II, 8, 16: PL 76, 1037.

(C) The second passage or paragraph 2, "By the charity . . . various religious communities," is taken over substantially from the previous draft with some additions or changes. It deals with the *ecclesiological* and *apostolic* aspects of the religious state, something that was insisted upon by the 679 fathers when they gave their views on the "sanctifying and redemptive value" of the religious state. Cf. E/1251, 1244 (79 bishops), 1258, 1270, 1323, 1230, etc. It now reads that this apostolic aim is to be achieved *in keeping with the form of their particular vocation.* This is why the subcommission also added at the end the words: "It is for this reason that the Church preserves and fosters the particular characteristics of the various institutes of Religious." All these things have been clarified and added, in compliance with the wish of the fathers, lest it appear that the apostolic aim is achieved only in one way, and lest those Religious who follow the life of contemplatives and of hermits seem to be despised. The ancient and recent ascetics either "occupy themselves with God alone" through contemplation, as St. Gregory the Great says in: *Dial.* I, 8: PL 77, 185, or they take on apostolic and charitable works over and above this, or they instruct the faithful in spiritual matters by serving as counselors.

The *spiritual fathers,* particularly in the East, belong to this last type. One can read about them, for example, in St. Basil the Great, *Serm. de renunt. saeculi,* 2: PG 31, 632 B: "Take special care in seeing to it that you find a man who will be a most safe guide for your life, one who has received sound training in giving guidance to those who are advancing toward God." The ancients put much stress upon rendering obedience toward such a director of one's conscience. See, for example: St. Basil the Great, *Serm. asc.* 2, 2, PG 31, col. 884 C; and *Constit. monast.* 19: col. 1387-1390. St. John Climacus, *Scala Parad.,* 4: PG 88, 706 BC. According to St. Thomas, 3 *Sent.,* Dist. 35, q. 1, a. 3, sol. 2, a knowledge of contemplation is a prerequisite to the active life, especially if one is to give exhortations. For contemplation ought to direct the active life. *Summa Theol.* II-II, q. 182, a. 4, ad 2.

(D) The third passage or paragraph 3, "The profession . . . the Holy Spirit," *is not found* in the previous draft in this form. It was added, however, in response to the wishes of those fathers who insist that the *Christological* and *eschatological* aspect of the religious state be elucidated. Besides being mentioned by the 679 fathers, this Christological and eschatological aspect was also mentioned in E/1053, 1108 (79 bishops), 1170, 1228, 1233, 1261, 1382, etc. The arrangement of the concepts is as follows: the religious state has *in addition* (therefore not exclusively, but after the preceding passages) the nature, the value, and the influence of a *sign* and of *testimony*. It is an eschatological sign, a sign of the earthly life of Christ, a sign of the urgent need for the Kingdom of God in the present life through the imitation of the virtues of Christ and through the power of the Holy Spirit. From this passage as a whole, however, there also shines forth an *apologetical* aspect of the religious state. For if in fact there are those who by the grace of God not only observe the precepts, but also *oblige* themselves to observe the counsels – and this perpetually and by vows – then it is not impossible to carry out the precepts of God.

(E) The last passage or last paragraph, "Thus, although . . . life and holiness," is not contained in the previous draft. But it corresponds to the desire expressed by many fathers, and serves as a conclusion to the nature and importance of the religious state. For the religious state is related to the very "pneuma" life of the Church and to its holiness. Compare, e.g., E/1189, 1229, 1326, 1328, 1387.

Therefore the religious state can and ought to become involved in all those things which pertain to the life of the Church. The following fathers among others made mention of this pre-eminence: E/1128, 1221, 1229, 1236, 1238, 1327, 1378, 1380, 1383, 1387 (26 bishops), etc.

> **COMMENT**: Abbott-Gallagher in this section speaks of "The religious state constitued by the profession of the evangelical

counsels." The word "religious" is not in the
official Latin text.

**Report on
Number 45**

Provisional title: Under the Authority of the Church.

(A) The first passage or paragraph 1, "Since it is . . .
in every way," is taken substantially from the previous
draft. The word *public,* however, has been deleted from
"public profession" in line number 21, lest the scope be
delimited. And the words *to explain faithfully* have also
been deleted from line 20, because this has already been
stated. The words *also when reinforced by vows* have
been added, in order to make mention right at this stage
of the vows of Religious.

> **COMMENT: Some further changes were
> made in the subsequent draft. See Qualifica-
> tions 35, page 88, and 38, page 89.**

Regarding the transition from the anchoritic life to
the *cenobitic* life, cf. Pius XII, Allocution *Nous sommes
heureux,* AAS 50 (1958) p. 284 f. The rules drawn up
for monasteries in the East and West by great founders,
e.g., Pachomius, Basil, Augustine, and Benedict, were approved by the Church and were made more specific as
time went on.

For praise of the monastic life, especially of the cenobitic life, cf. St. Gregory Nazianzen, *Orat.* 6, 2: PG 35,
721 ff; ibid, 21, 19: col. 1101 f; *Orat.* 43, 62: PG 36,
576. St. John Chrysostom, *Adv. oppugn. vitam monast.,*
3, 11: PG 47, 366. St. Nilus, *Epist.* 3, 33: PG 79, 388 ff.
St. Jerome, *Epist.* 125, 15: PL 22, 1080 f. Theodoret,
Religiosa Hist., 5: PG 82, 1353.

Cassian, in his *Instit.* II, 5: PL 49, 84-88, and in his

Collat. 18, 5: col. 1094 B - 1100 A, deduces monasticism from the pristine "apostolic" community, according to Eusebius of Caesarea, *Eccl. Hist.* II, 17: PG 20, 173-184. This affirmation is accepted, not on the basis of historical continuity, but on the basis of some sort of spiritual filiation.

(B) The second passage or paragraph 2, "Any institute . . . unity and harmony," is taken substantially from the previous draft. But there are some additions, like the words: *can be left or committed to the charge of their proper patriarchical authorities.* These words have been added in view of the Oriental Church and the power that patriarchs have over Religious. Compare, e.g., E/1238, 1378. The text referring to the Supreme Pontiff reads: "by virtue of his *primacy over the universal Church,"* and not "by virtue of full and supreme power." For this latter expression can also be applied to the council or to the body of bishops, whereas "primacy" holds for the Pontiff alone. The 679 fathers insist on this "being at the disposal of" the Supreme Pontiff; compare also, E/1253, 1265, 1273, 1386 (55 bishops). The words of Pius XII on the *concord and cooperation* to be shown by religious in the apostolate, are taken from his Allocution *Annus sacer,* AAS 43 (1951) p. 28, and are copied from footnote 20 on page 28 of the 1963 draft of this chapter.

(C) The third passage or last paragraph, "By her approval . . . Eucharistic sacrifice," is *new.* It was introduced to satisfy a certain father E/1177, who requested that the role of liturgy in religious profession should be indicated, lest it appear that the whole of the Church's activity is expended only on the juridical aspect of the state of Religious.

41

Report on
Number 46

Provisional title: Consecration through the Evangelical Counsels Ought to be Appreciated.

(A) A new draft has been made by using the previous text with some parts being changed and others omitted. In the title itself the expression *consecration* is used in place of the word *profession,* because *consecration* is broader and includes also those who have no vows. Further, the first passage of the previous text has been omitted, because the principle has already been stated in some way — and in fact more concisely — at the beginning of Number 43. The topic being treated here is the appreciation that ought to be shown for the religious state, both by Religious themselves and by others. Consequently:

(B) The first passage or paragraph 1, "Religious . . . who sent Him," is taken from the previous draft, with some changes. Among them, the expression *to believers and non-believers alike* has been added, in order to stress the missionary aim of some religious institutes.

(C) The second passage or part 1 of paragraph 2, "Finally . . . Mother also chose," is taken from the previous draft. Some amendments have been made. For example, *by its very nature* has been inserted before "it is most beneficial," in order to point out that the religious state of itself tends toward genuine development of the human person, even though this may not come about in some individual cases because of accidental occurrences or because of various circumstances. Likewise *voluntarily* has been introduced into the text in connection with "a vocation given to him personally," in order to express in this way that the personality has asserted itself through a *voluntary* act. In place of "to the purification of human affections" (of the previous draft), which savors of "the apathy" of the Stoics, there has been substituted "to purification *of heart.*" "Followed," at the end, has been changed to "embraced," since this is the more appropriate word. After "to bring into conformity" has been added *are effective;* we thus look forward to a final goal, rather than affirm as a fact what sometimes happens not to come about. Some words have been added on saintly *founders.* However, the words "in charity" (of the previous draft) and "for promoting human society in various ways" have been deleted, since they are not necessary. There are also some other textual changes of minor importance.

> **COMMENT**: This particular section in Abbott-Gallagher is quite defective. "Poor life" is translated as "humble life," "embraced" as "chose," "proves" as "shows," and the word "more" is missing in a strategic place. The following might prove acceptable as an alternative translation: "For when anyone has voluntarily taken up the practice of the counsels according to the dictates of a vocation given to him personally, these counsels contribute in no small way to his purification of heart and to making him free for spiritual things. They also provide a constant stimulant for keeping charity fervent. Further, as the example of so many saintly founders proves, the counsels are especially effective in bringing a Christian man or woman more into conformity with that kind

43

of virginal and poor life, which Christ Our
Lord chose for Himself and which His Virgin
Mother also embraced."

(D) The third passage or part 2 of paragraph 2, "Let
no one . . . labored in vain," affirms that the religious
state contributes *to the cultivation of one's personality.*
The Religious renounces for himself, it is true, temporal
goods, family life and his own will, but only for the sake
of God, the highest value there is. And he does this
because God Himself invites him and spurs on his spirit.
Through this kind of prompt abnegation on his part he
removes the impediments that retard charity, namely,
the threefold concupiscence (cf. 1 John 2, 16), and he
acquires precious freedom for serving God and his brothers.

The fathers of the Church exalt this freedom, e.g., St.
Cyprian, *De Dom. Orat.* 20: PL 4, 551 B: "That one, he
says, can follow Him and imitate the glory of the Lord's
Passion who is unimpeded and ready for anything, not
being involved with difficulties connected with house-
hold affairs. But being unattached and free, he himself
follows after his possessions, having sent them on ahead
to God."

St. Jerome, *Epist.* 108, 15: PL 22, 892; "That one
(namely Paula) being more ardent in faith was attached
to the Savior with her whole mind. And being poor in
spirit, she followed Our Lord Who was poor, giving Him
what she had received, being made poor for His sake."

St. Jerome, *Epist.* 125, 20: PL 22, Col. 1085: "If you
wish to be perfect, go with Abraham out of your coun-
try and away from your relatives, and head for some
unknown destination. If you own possessions, sell them
and give the price to the poor. If you have no posses-

sions, you have been freed from a great burden; being naked yourself you can follow the naked Christ. It is hard, it is much to ask, it is difficult; but the rewards are great."

St. Nilus, *De octo spir. mal.* 7: PG 79, 1152 B: "The monk who has many possessions is a ship weighed down with much freight, and when a storm comes up at sea he easily sinks. For just like a ship with an overflowing bilge is awash with every wave, so one who has many possessions is submerged by his anxieties. The monk without a possession is an unimpeded traveler and finds lodging everywhere. The monk who possesses nothing is an eagle soaring to lofty heights, who takes time out from his flight for nourishment only when forced by necessity."

Compare St. Thomas, *Contra Gentiles,* III, 130; *Summa Theol.* I-II, q. 108, a. 4; *ibid.,* II-II, q. 184, a. 3; *Contra retrah. a relig. ingressu,* cap. 6; *Quodl.* 4, a. 24. P. Philippe, O.P., *Les fins de la vie religieuse selon S. Thomas,* Rome 1962, especially pages 32 ff.

Pius XII in his Allocution *Annus sacer,* 8 December 1950, AAS 43 (1951) p. 30, teaches that the religious state has not been provided as a haven of safety for the timid and for those with anxieties. On the contrary, he says it demands a magnanimous spirit and earnestness in applying oneself, as is clearly manifest from history. Again, in his Allocution *Sous la maternelle protection,* 9 December 1957, AAS 50 (1958) p. 39 f., he teaches that the religious life does not inculcate infantilism, but that it augments the perfection and personal dignity of an adult person through the practice of charity.

(E) The last passage and paragraph, "In summary every variety," was taken from the previous draft — after a few deletions were made. One such deletion was the word "innumerable" in the phrase *"innumerable men and women, Brothers and Sisters."* The following phrase, however, was added: *in monasteries, or in schools and hospitals, or on the missions,* in order to give praise and honor to those who are simply Brothers and Sisters and who labor so much for Christ and the Church without having the honor of the priesthood.

Report on Number 47

Provisional title: Conclusion

(A) The sentence "In summary . . . every variety," taken from Number 36 of the previous draft has been transferred with a few changes to Number 46 of the present draft.

(B) The passage, "Let each one . . . wellspring of all holiness," has likewise been taken from the previous draft, after the initial words were dropped: "For since the faithful are obliged to aspire after holiness in an evangelical spirit." These words were omitted because they pertain rather to that part of the schema which treats of holiness. The *Most Holy Trinity* is called the fountain of holiness at the end of the passage; naturally this means through *Christ.*

Chapter Four

AN ADDITIONAL REPORT

Chapter Four
AN ADDITIONAL REPORT[9]

In addition to the individual wishes of the fathers proposed to the council, there exists a document signed by 679 fathers that was transmitted to the Doctrinal Commission by the Supreme Pontiff in order that "its value might be determined after a diligent examination." In this document the request is made that chapter V (once IV) be divided in two, so that there be *a special chapter on Religious.* Certain others have joined their voices to those of the 679 fathers.

On the other hand there were very many who preferred a *single continuous exposition* on Holiness and on Religious, as 254 fathers explicitly declared, while very many others wished to retain the previous draft that had been approved in the Council Hall as a basis of discussion. Their total number probably surpassed 500.

Organization of Material

It will be profitable for the fathers if we summarize the arguments presented by both sides in favor of the two different ways of organizing the material.

Separate Chapter on Religious

A separate chapter on Religious is requested in the document of the 679 fathers for these general reasons:

a) because of the *special place* that belongs to Religious in the Church in view of the way in which the Church is constituted;

---

[9] **Ibid.,** pp. 174-177.

b) because of the very great *importance of the presence* of Religious in the Church and because of the typical function they perform in it;

c) because in such a chapter *all the aspects* can be explained regarding the presence in the Church of those who effectively profess the evangelical counsels.

Their specific reasons, which in more than one case partially include one another, are as follows:

1. The treatment of the special holiness and common holiness in a single chapter leads to *promiscuousness in composing the text,* something that seems to be founded on rather recent and controverted opinions which are neither certain nor clear; thus, E/1327. Compare E/1270.

Logical order requires that the purpose — that is to say the holiness — of the People of God be treated first. Afterwards treatment should be given to particulars, that is, to the different roles and states of life; thus E/1257. The laity are also being treated under a special heading; both historical and ecumenical reasons require the same treatment for Religious; thus E/1181, (21 fathers). Whereas the laity bring about "the consecration of the world" through their presence and through their Christian activity in it, the Religious not only privately but publicly as well manifest the Kingdom of God, which is not of this world. They do this through their effective renunciation of earthly things; thus E/1326. The reality of the religious life cannot be limited here to the single aspect of a call to holiness, lest this make religious vocations dwindle even more; thus E/1384 (6 fathers). Therefore *in order to avoid confusion* let there be separate treatment of the consecrated life as was done in the past; thus E/1255. The evangelical counsels are not only means for fostering holiness, but means for promoting the Kingdom of Heaven in every way possible. In view of this consideration, the entire breadth of the mission of the Church should be indicated, and not only the one dimension of holiness; thus E/1381.

2. Treatment in a single chapter would create the impression that today the Church, so to say, *no longer has a high appreciation* of the religious life; this in turn would cause great damage to the Church and would make our separated brethren wonder; thus E/1386. The same thing was said by E/1328, who also fears that the state of perfection would *depreciates*; and he calls attention to the high esteem which the Orientals have for the monastic life. As is further said by E/1253, the treatment given to Religious, therefore, must not be contained *in an aside,* as if it were being mentioned just by the way. Nor ought it to be treated *only casually* in some general chapter on holiness; thus E/1258. Fostering *less esteem*, indifferentism, and laxism, and promoting the activity of innovators who are striving to bring all Religious to a common level, is something unlawful and something counter to the rights which Religious have — rights that are recognized in the Church; thus E/1162. In order to keep the theme of Religious from *being obscured,* as E/1203 admonishes, its *excellence* and importance ought to be extolled; thus E/1147. Therefore the text ought to speak properly, candidly and explicitly also *about the fruitful activity* of Religious for the life of the Church — something that is evident, for example, from the fact that their number is so immense; thus E/980. The *pre-eminence* of this state, therefore, ought not to be diminished; thus E/1223.

3. For centuries now it has been acknowledged that

Religious constitute *"a state"* in the Church. Although this state does not pertain to the divine institution of the Church, it nevertheless does pertain essentially to the life of the Church, and is also a constituent element in the Church's mark of holiness; thus E/1221. Hence there must be recognized a two-fold calling to holiness; this recognition will prove advantageous for Religious and for the Church itself; thus E/1290. The state of Religious *is not incidental* to the Church, but as a state is the opposite of the laity in the world; thus E/1291.

4. Although common holiness and the holiness of the states of perfection are, simply speaking, both the same, they nevertheless do differ by *degree;* otherwise there would be no reason for embracing and recommending the state of perfection; thus E/1334. It is not pedagogically sound to treat of perfection in general together with religious perfection in a single chapter, because this minimizes and obscures the state of Religious, since it does not bring out the specific and theological characteristics of their state; thus E/1234.

> **COMMENT: The word "same" as used in this proposal was not adopted by the Doctrinal Commission, which said that holiness was *one* for the lay state and for the religious state, but *not* the same. Cf. The General Report, page 21, f.**

5. The state of perfection is *substantially of divine institution;* it stems from Christ's will, not by way of precept, but by way of counsel. The state of perfection creates a distinction in the Church, not on the basis of the Church as an hierarchical society, but on the basis of the Church as a spiritual society directed toward holiness. The state of perfection is found in a germinal stage

in the gospel and in the practice of the primitive Church, and there is also evidence of some organic evolution, just as in the case of the episcopacy and the priesthood. The state of perfection is the perfect imitation of Christ which cannot be lacking to the Church. Thus E/1328. Besides the division into hierarchy and laity, there is also *by the will of Christ* the two-fold category of those who are called to practice the counsels effectively and totally, and of others who are not; thus E/1176 (25 fathers).

As regards the *place* where the section on universal holiness ought to be inserted, the document of the 679 fathers suggests the chapter on the People of God, or also the chapter on the Mystery of the Church. Among the fathers who individually treated this issue, very many prefer to have it inserted in the chapter on the People of God: E/522 (22 fathers), E/980, 1147, 1162, 1181 (21 fathers), 1214, 1253 (5 fathers), 1255, 1257, 1270, 1290, 1326, 1328, 1364 (11 fathers). Others, however, prefer the chapter on the Mystery of the Church: E/550, 1131, 1178, 1208, 1213, 1382.

Single Chapter on Holiness and Religious

Those in favor of *a continuous exposition in a single chapter,* divided however into two sections, gave the following reasons:

1. E/1057 (58 fathers): They would like to have the life of the counsels treated in an ecclesial context together with the universal call to holiness:

a) for at times the faithful have the conviction that *holiness is reserved* for Religious or priests alone, something which of course does not fail to have bad consequences on the Christian life of the faithful;

b) in this way the life of the counsels will look more like a charism for providing the Christian community with *eschatological testimony;*

c) thus the religious state is not presented as something juridical, but rather as a charismatic life always existing in the Church and proceeding from her essence. Thus also E/518 (30 fathers).

2. E/1058: The first reason is *theological:* the distinction between clergy and laity pertains to the constitutive structure of the Church and strictly speaking is by divine right; Religious, however, constitute a structure *in* the Church and not the structure of the Church. The second reason is *pastoral:* the impression that perfection and holiness are a quasi monopoly reserved for Religious must be removed; hence it would be of great help to present the religious life in the perspective of the universal call to holiness. The third reason is *ecumenical:* the leaders of the Protestant Reformation had intended to destroy the wall which they considered erected by the Church between the faithful and Religious, as if these latter were called to a higher holiness and to holiness properly so called, whereas the others were called only to elementary salvation. This erroneous interpretation must be prudently corrected through the structure of this chapter.

3. E/1108 (79 fathers): They would like to have the evangelical counsels and the profession of them considered in a theological context which includes the people as a whole. By treating of a call to holiness which all the faithful have, one can efficaciously refute the false opinion of those who reproach the Church for harboring in her breast according to her

ascetical doctrine *two classes of Christians,* some with more and some with less perfection, depending upon the state in which they live. Others also give their support to this consideration, arguing that Religious do not have a quasi monopoly on perfection; thus E/1292; nor do Religious constitute a kind of aristocracy; thus E/1245; nor ought they to be separated from the rest of the church because of their "ideal" of perfection; thus E/1053.

4. E/1055:

a) If this material is transferred to the chapter *on the People of God,* more things would be thrown *into confusion* because of it; thus, for example, the counsels would have to be treated twice: for the ones who practice the counsels privately and for those who make a public profession of them.

b) Striving for holiness ought to appear as the *culmination of the entire schema;* hence it is requested that the various methods and various paths to holiness be combined in a single chapter, which would treat of various groups, and also of Religious in a very special way.

c) If Religious are separated from the rest of the members of the Church in this exposition, their significance in the Church would no longer appear in its proper light; the impression would be created as if they constituted some species not closely enough joined with the people who make up the faithful, and the institutional *manifestation* of acquiring holiness *would be diminished* greatly. On the other hand, namely: if they are placed in the literary and doctrinal context of the entire

Church, we can rightly hope that both the number of vocations and the perseverance of the candidates will increase.

5. E/1170: The role of those who are Religious is *to serve as a sign* and *to give testimony* on behalf of the Kingdom of God and the new life in Christ; this meaning must be inculcated in the schema. The most suitable place to do this is in the chapter on the universal call to holiness; this will not be to the detriment of Religious, but *in their favor.*

Certain fathers who, as has been said, were joined by many others, propose that the tract with two parts have a *title* almost like this: "On the Universal Call to Holiness, and Especially on Religious." For the second part of the title others prefer to say: "Those Who Profess the Evangelical Counsels," or "on the States of Perfection."

The subcommission and the plenary commission, however, decided to speak simply "of Religious," lest one become engaged in theological controversies on the innermost essence of the religious state, as will be explained in further detail later.

Chapter Five

CONCLUSIONS OF THE DOCTRINAL COMMISSION

Chapter Five

CONCLUSIONS OF
THE DOCTRINAL COMMISSION[10]

The matter was at this stage when in the joint sub-commission meeting of January 28, 1964, the following compromise was reached, and was approved by the Doctrinal Commission in plenary session in March:

1) Whatever is done, the exposition on holiness and on Religious *should be divided into two parts,* which will be presented either as two Chapters (V and VI), or as two sections of one Chapter (V. A and V. B). The settlement of this latter question is left to the council itself. On the basis of a provisional consultation it was evident that the majority of the members of the joint subcommission tended toward two chapters, and the minority toward two sections of one chapter (7 members to 4).

2) *All* were in agreement that *the organization of the material as a whole in the exposition should not be changed,* particularly because the transferal of the section on Holiness to the chapter on the People of God could not be accomplished without great inconvenience and very much work. Many parts of the text, already approved, would have to be revised again according to the new succession of ideas. It was therefore preferred that the principal of the universal call to holiness should be treated in Chapter V (or V. A), and that the special call to the Religious state should be treated in Chapter

---

[10] Ibid., pp. 177-179

VI (or V. B). In the chapter *on the People of God,* however, *certain things were to be inserted by way of anticipation* concerning the call to perfect holiness which all the faithful have, whatever their condition or state of life — this has been done at the end of Number 11; and concerning the various ranks in the Church — this has been done in Number 13, paragraph 3. The various ranks result either from a difference in duties (clergy-laity) or from a difference in the condition and orientation of one's life (religious-laity).

> **COMMENT: For the first reference see the last paragraph of Number 11 in Abbott-Gallagher, page 29. For the second reference see the paragraph on the bottom of page 40.**

3) If the general sequence of the material under discussion is retained, *there will not be any disturbance in the logical exposition.* For although distinctions are generally made as if there were three states in the Church, namely: of clerics, of religious, and of laity, everyone knows that this division into three states arises from the twofold distinction which has its basis — so to say — in two different planes. And so it is clear that both the clergy and the laity can enter the religious state.

The distinction existing *between hierarchy and people* arises from the divine institution of ecclesiastical authority, and is founded in the fact that certain ones receive the character of Orders over and above the character of Baptism. The distinction existing *between Religious and others,* however, arises from the difference between a universal call and a particular call. This difference is based on the way that each one must follow his call in striving for holiness in view of the gift that he has received. The life of an effective profession of the counsels pertains to the goal and to the life of the Church and it prefigures the life of the Kingdom of Heaven, where the chosen will neither marry nor be given in marriage (cf. Matt. 22, 30). Thus, E/1326.

Therefore, just as the chapter on the laity corresponds to the chapter that describes the institution of the hierarchy, so too the exposition on the special way to be followed by the *religious state* corresponds to the exposition on the universal call to holiness.

This consideration, already referred to in reasons 3 and 5 of the first set of arguments given above, is corroborated by pontifical documents, which are quoted in the paper by the same E/1326.

Pius XII, Apostolic Constitution, *Provida Mater,* 2 February 1947: AAS 39 (1947), p. 116: "Moreover the other two ranks of canonical persons, namely the clerics and the laity, are exacted from the Church by divine right in so far as the Church is a society hierarchically constituted and organized. In addition to this they have been instituted by the Church; cf. canons 107, 108 § 3. *The class of Religious,* however, which is *midway* between the clergy and the laity, can be common both to the clergy and to the laity (canon 107), and derives completely *from its close and peculiar relationship to the goal of the Church, namely holiness.* One ought to strive for this goal efficaciously and by taking adequate measures."

Pius XII, Allocution, *Annus sacer,* 8 December 1950: AAS 43 (1951), p. 27-28: "Divine right itself has established that the clergy are distinguished from the laity. Placed between these two grades is the state of the religious life. This state, *coming about through ecclesiastical origin, exists precisely – and has value precisely – be-*

cause of the fact that it is intimately bound up with the Church's own aim, which is that men may be led to acquire *holiness."*

The arrangement of the entire Schema on the Church would therefore be as follows:

Chapter I, entitled *The Mystery of the Church,* describes the divine origin of the Church and its inmost nature.

Added to this is Chapter II, entitled *The People of God,* which rather concisely explains the pilgrimage of the new People here on earth. It tells the role of the People in the exercise of the common priesthood, draws attention to the sense of faith and to the charisms, and sets forth catholic or universal unity of the People. Relationships with various categories of Christians and of men in general are also explained.

Chapter III takes up *the Hierarchical Constitution of the Church,* by virtue of which Bishops by their sacramental consecration become successors of the Apostles. They together with their head the Supreme Pontiff constitute a Body or Order and, with the assistance of priests and deacons, exercise various ministries, namely those of teaching, sanctifying and ruling.

Then in Chapter IV it is taught that the Christian dignity of the laity is not only not lessened by the Church's hierarchical constitution, but it is confirmed. Thus the laity under the leadership of the hierarchy can collaborate in the saving mission of the Church under the aspect of the above threefold ministry in a spirit of Christian obedience and trusting concord.

After an exposition of "the hierarchical constitution" the schema expressly turns its attention to the "goal" toward which the Church tends and in Chapter V treats *of the Call that everyone has to Holiness* and to perfection, which are to be sought under various forms and in diverse categories. The ways and means also differ, according to each one's vocation, and the evangelical counsels are not excluded.

In Chapter VI (or V. B), moreover, a precise explanation is given of the state of those – namely *Religious* – who under ecclesiastical authority effectively put the evangelical counsels into practice. Their total consecration to God leads to a closer and more exact imitation of Christ. Likewise, the ecclesial and eschatological importance of this state is manifested, esteem for it is inculcated, and its fruitful activity is explained.

Chapter VII (or VI) next treats specifically of the *consummation of holiness* in the glory of the Saints in heaven, and of the union that exists between us and them.

And finally in Chapter VIII (or VII) there is special consideration given to the Blessed Virgin Mary, both in the mystery of Christ, whose mother she is, and in the mystery of the Church, whose maternal and virginal type she is. In this final chapter, which serves as a crown, one could say the whole exposition on the Mystery of the Church has been summarized.

Chapter Six

THE GENERAL ASSEMBLY VOTES

Chapter Six

THE GENERAL ASSEMBLY VOTES

COMMENT: On September 30, 1964, sixteen days after the opening of the third session of Vatican II, a ballot was taken on the question: "Should there be a special chapter on Religious?" Since it was a matter of procedure, 50 per cent of the votes plus one were required for passage. The results were these:

Yes:	1505
No:	698
Void:	7
Total:	2210[11]

The ballot left no doubt, and at this moment, a separate chapter on Religious formally came into being.

A single ballot was also taken that day on the acceptability of the newly revised paragraphs Numbers 43, 44, 45, 46 and 47. One could vote in favor of the text, or against it; or in favor of it *with qualifications* (technically called *modi.*) These qualifications or amendments had to be submitted in writing at the time of voting, and there was no limit to the number of qualifications that a council father could submit. But for passage, the

---

[11] Schema Constitutionis Dogmaticae De Ecclesia: Modi a Commissione Doctrinali Examinati A Patribus Conciliaribus Propositi; IV: Capita IV, V: De Laicis – De Universali Vocatione ad Sanctitatem in Ecclesia (Polyglot Press, Vatican City, 1964), p. 17.

text which now was in its third draft needed a two-thirds majority of affirmative votes *without* qualifications. The results were as follows:

Yes:	1736
Yes (with qualifications):	438
No:	12
Void:	3
Total:	2189[12]

These returns meant that technically speaking the Doctrinal Commission was free to ignore the qualifications submitted by the 438 council fathers, because 79 per cent of the assembly had cast unqualified affirmative votes. The returns also meant that the assembly was ready to accept chapter VI on Religious, with all its parts, just as it now stood.

But council commissions regularly gave careful attention to all qualifications submitted by the fathers, and the Doctrinal Commission made no exception in this case. First it assigned a subcommission to examine the qualifications, and later examined them in a plenary session. As the council fathers were informed by the Doctrinal Commission, the preliminary examination was made "by Most Rev. Father Butler in place of the Most Rev. Father Gut, Relator of Chapter VI, who had been hindered from taking charge in these days, and by the secretaries of the Doctrinal Commission, under the presidency of Most

---

[12] Schema Constitutionis Dogmaticae De Ecclesia: Modi a Patribus Conciliaribus Propositi a Commissione Doctrinali Examinati; V: Caput VI De Religiosis (Polyglot Press, Vatican City, 1964), p. 3.

Rev. Charue, delegated by the President of the Doctrinal Commission."

The results of this study and the decisions reached by the Doctrinal Commission in plenary session were prepared for distribution to the council fathers.

Chapter Seven

QUALIFICATIONS AND REPLIES: ON RELIGIOUS

Chapter Seven

QUALIFICATIONS AND REPLIES: ON RELIGIOUS[13]

COMMENT: On November 14, 1964, one week before the end of the third session, the council fathers received a large but thin booklet of 14 pages. Its contents will be examined in this chapter. Under fifty headings were contained all the qualifications that had been submitted by the 438 council fathers in the voting that took place the previous September 30. In each case, after listing a group of related qualifications, the Doctrinal Commission gave its reply, indicating this with the letter "R". It rejected the vast majority of qualifications, but accepted some. The first six headings contained qualifications of a general nature; under the other headings were specific points which referred to Numbers 43, 44, 45, 46 or 47 of the Chapter on Religious.

In General

1 — Seven Fathers see difficulties in the title of the chapter as given on page 155. (The title was "Religious.") These difficulties arise especially from the unsuitability of including secular institutions under the name "Religious," and also from the existence of forms of consecration which are made without vows (e.g., that of hermits). Four fathers propose that the title be: "The

---

[13] Ibid., pp. 3-14

Profession of the Evangelical Counsels in the Church";
two others suggest: "The Consecrated," or "The Faithful Consecrated to God." Another suggests: "The (Particular) State of Evangelical Perfection in the Church"; and still another suggests: "The Evangelical Counsels." And last of all, two ask that the words "Religious" and "Religious Life" be completely avoided.

> **COMMENT: "Page 155" was the first page of the third draft of the chapter on Religious, on which the council fathers had voted. The chapter covered pages 155-159. See pages 115-131 of this book, where these pages are reprinted.**

R — After the Doctrinal Commission found that the commission on Religious was in agreement, it decided to use the general term *Religious* without entering into further specifications.

2 — Pages 155 ff: One father requests that this entire chapter should be improved by including the more outstanding sentences of His Holiness Paul VI's Allocution of May 23, 1964.

R — Longer quotations cannot be included. Exact references to the Allocution of His Holiness Paul VI are made in the footnotes.

> **COMMENT: Inclusions made in footnotes also became official teaching of the Vatican Council, in so far as these footnotes qualified the main text. The footnotes were subject to amendment just like the text itself.**

3 — Pages 155 ff: One father insists on keeping the suggestion that he submitted in writing earlier regarding the mutual relations of Religious and local ordinaries.

R — Provision has been made for this in Number 28, page 73, lines 39 ff. We cannot enter here into juridical questions.

> **COMMENT: This text in Abbott-Gallagher begins on page 54, seven lines from the bottom: "All priests, both diocesan and religious . . ."**

4 – Pages 155 ff: One father asks that *there be added* a new paragraph about religious life *in the Missions,* with the view of inculcating the necessity of forming an autochthonous religious clergy.

R – A better place for treating this topic is the schema on the Missions.

> **COMMENT: This was done in Number 18 of the Decree on the Church's Missionary Activity. Cf. Abbott-Gallagher, pages 606-607.**

5 – Pages 155 ff: One father proposes that those things which express the *ecclesiological* aspect of the state of perfection (e.g. the major part of Number 43 and Number 47) should be transferred to Chapter V (on the Universal Call to Holiness), whereas the other parts of Chapter VI (on Religious) belong strictly speaking to the schema on Religious.

> **COMMENT: "Schema on Religious" here means the document that eventually became the *Decree on the Appropriate Renewal of the Religious Life.***

R – For practical reasons a new structure cannot be realized.

6 – Pages 155 ff: Two fathers propose that almost all of Chapter VI (on Religious) together with Chapter V (on the Universal Call to Holiness) should follow Chapter II, on the People of God. Only those points which pertain to the juridical structure of the religious state

should be left here where they are.

R — The reply is the same as that for Qualification 5.

Number 43

7 — Page 155, lines 1 ff: One father asks why in the very beginning of the schema reference is made to *the evangelical counsels,* whereas the primordial reason for the religious state is found in *the consecration to God,* sanctioned in a special way by the Church.

R — The text will remain as it is. *Consecration* is explicitly treated in Number 44, page 156, lines 12 ff.

> **COMMENT: This text on "consecration" in Abbott-Gallagher begins seven lines from the bottom on page 74: "Thus he is more intimately consecrated . . ."**

8 — Page 155, lines 2-4: Three fathers ask for the deletion of the words: "of chastity dedicated to God, poverty, and obedience," because they seem to exclude the life of hermits and new forms of religious life which can arise in younger Churches.

> **COMMENT: Cf. Abbott-Gallagher, the first two lines on page 73.**

R — A general description is in question here. Also, hermits in their own way profess the counsels. Explicit mention of hermits is made in line 14 on the same page.

> **COMMENT: Cf. Abbott-Gallagher, page 73, line 11.**

9 — Page 155, line 3: Two fathers wish to have the words "chastity dedicated to God" changed to "celibacy for the sake of the kingdom of heaven." The former words are not Biblical; and besides the chastity of both

the unmarried as well as the married is dedicated to God. One father proposes that "virginal chastity" should be added.

R — These proposals are not accepted.

10 — Page 155, line 9: One father proposes the insertion of this definition of the religious life, which includes all institutes of perfection: "The religious state is a way of living, recognized by the Church, whereby the faithful consecrate their own life to God in a special way in order to achieve the perfection of charity in the service of the Church."

R — Because strict "definitions" are very difficult, especially when very many elements are still controverted, the Commission intentionally abstained from giving "definitions," both for the word "laity" and for the word "Religious."

11 — Page 155, lines 9-11: Four fathers propose that "To interpret them (i.e., the evangelical counsels), to regulate their practice, as well as to found stable forms of living according to them is also its (i.e., the Church's) concern," should be substituted with another sentence, because an historical narration is in question here. They suggest: "The hierarchical Church has indeed regulated the practice of them and also has sanctioned stable forms of living according to them." The interpreting of the counsels as well, in accord naturally with the regulations made by the hierarchy, has often been done by the founders themselves. Another father asks that the text be made to read: "It is really the concern of the magisterium of the Church . . . ," because in line 7 the word "Church" has a universal sense.

R — The historical description does not begin until

line 11 ("Thus it has come about, . . . etc."). Line 9 will be revised to read as follows: "The *authority* of the Church itself, moreover, *under the guidance of the Holy Spirit, has taken care* to interpret, . . . etc."

> **COMMENT: The translation of line 9 as given in Abbott-Gallagher on page 73, lines 7-8, is somewhat faulty. The Latin reads:** *Ipsa autem auctoritas Ecclesiae, duce Spiritu Sancto, ea interpretari . . . curavit.* **(The English translation is under the preceding "R.")**

12 – Page 155, line 11: Seven fathers ask for the following addition taken from the first schema *On the Church* (ed. 1962, Chapter V, page 32, lines 29 ff): " . . . to found stable forms of living according to them. For certainly the grace of the Holy Spirit never stops urging many of the faithful to begin leading the life of the heavenly Jerusalem in so far as this is possible in the flesh, and to strive also to imitate Christ more closely. Thus it has come about . . ." This improves the connection between the ideas, calls to mind the influence of the Holy Spirit, and also makes allusion right at the beginning to the eschatological aspect and to the purpose of this vocation, namely, the imitation of Christ.

R – As for the Holy Spirit, this has already been provided for under Qualification 11. The other elements will be treated later.

13 – Page 155, line 15: One father requests that after the words "various forms of solitary or community life," there be added: "or of life in the world itself as members of some profession" or something similar to this, because of the secular institutes.

R – This idea is not denied in the text as it stands.

Mention is explicitly made of *various forms*.

14 – Page 155, lines 18-25: Five fathers have proposed a rather lengthy amplification which deals as well with community life in the pristine Church.

> **COMMENT: For the passage in question, confer Abbott-Gallagher, page 73, last line, and page 74, first six lines.**

R – There is no need for such a particularized description.

15 – Page 155, line 22: One father proposes that in place of "liberty amplified through obedience" the text should read: "multiple helps springing from obedience"; three others however propose: "liberty confirmed (or strengthened) through obedience," because the word "amplified" seems too subtle.

R – *"Strengthened"* will be used in place of *"amplified"*.

> **COMMENT: In Abbott-Gallagher, page 73, the word "support" in the last line seems to go only with "greater stability". Ambiguity could be avoided by translating the Latin as follows: "These religious families give their members the following support: greater stability . . . a proven method . . . etc."**

16 – Page 155, line 25: After the words: "make progress on the road of charity," 372 fathers wish to have added the following passage from Pope Paul VI's Allocution to Religious of May 23, 1964: *"The characteristic of this state, which receives its particular excellence from the profession of the evangelical vows (sic!), is that perfect manner of living according to the example and teachings of Jesus Christ, which strives to increase charity and bring it to perfection."*

R — A reference to the Allocution of His Holiness Paul VI is being added to Footnote 2. The ideas, however, have already been indicated in the text approved earlier.

> **COMMENT: According to this "Reply" the reference was to be included in Footnote 211 in Abbott-Gallagher, page 74. But eventually Footnote 210 was created for it alone, *ibid.*; the footnote was inserted precisely at the spot requested by the 372 council fathers.**

17 — Page 155, lines 26-32: One father asks that this entire paragraph be deleted.

> **COMMENT: In Abbott-Gallagher the text referred to is on page 74, lines 7 to 13.**

R — This is not in accordance with the norms.

18 — Page 155, line 29: One father points out that rarely do clerics embrace the religious state; it usually happens the other way around. He therefore suggests that the text read: "But whether or not they enter service as clerics, some of Christ's faithful are called by God . . ."

R — This specification is not necessary.

> **COMMENT: In Abbott-Gallagher, page 74, "some of" should be inserted at the beginning of line 10: "Rather, *some of* the faithful of Christ . . . etc." The Latin has: *quidam christifideles.***

19 — Page 155: Two fathers ask that the following footnote be added to this Number 43: "What is said in this chapter about the religious life being so exemplary ought to be understood in an assertive and not in an exclusive sense," since priests and laity can also give

good example.

R – This has already been provided for in Chapter V on the universal call to holiness.

Number 44

20 – Page 156, passim: Fifteen fathers ask that the terminology be altered in such a way in all of Number 44 that the word "vows" be no longer the only word used, but that either "bonds" (in Latin: *vincula*) or "ties" (in Latin: *ligamina*) be used as an alternate word. Or one could simply substitute for "vows" the phrase "profession of the evangelical counsels" (9 fathers). *Reason*: Otherwise the members of societies *without vows* may come to think that they are not meant in this entire Number 44.

R – Let the texts be altered as follows:

Line 2: "By vows, *or by other sacred ties which in their own particular way are similar to vows,* a believer in Christ obliges himself to observe the three previously mentioned evangelical counsels. Through these same vows or ties he gives himself so totally to God, whom he loves above all else, that he becomes committed to God's service and to His honor by a new and special title."

> **COMMENT: The reader would do well to use this above translation instead of paragraph 1, Number 44, page 74, in Abbott-Gallagher, where the translation is quite faulty.**

Line 10: *"by the profession of the evangelical counsels in the Church* he has the intention of being freed from . . ."

> **COMMENT: The text in Abbott-Gallagher is on page 74, Number 44, lines 9-10. Before**

being amended the text read: *"by taking vows* he has the intention . . ."

Line 13: Delete: "by these same vows."

COMMENT: For this passage see: Abbott-Gallagher, page 74, Number 44, line 13. Before being amended the text read: " . . . he is more intimately consecrated *by these same vows* to divine service." Abbott-Gallagher has made this sentence stand by itself. But lines 7-13 in Number 44 would more correctly be translated from the final Latin text as follows:

"It is true that through Baptism he has died to sin and has *become dedicated* to God. By profession of the evangelical counsels in the Church, however, he intends *to be freed from obstacles which could* draw him away from the fervor of charity and the perfection of divine worship, and he is more intimately consecrated to divine service. He does this, moreover, in order *to be able* to derive more abundant fruit from his baptismal grace."

Note that all words in italics here are either different from or missing in the Abbott-Gallagher translation. The Latin text distinguishes between the *dedication* effected through Baptism (in Latin: Per baptismum . . . est . . . Deo *sacratus*) and the *consecration* effected through profession of the evangelical counsels (in Latin: consiliorum evangelicorum professione in Ecclesia . . . divino obsequio intimius *consecratur*). Thus it is evident that, although "by these same vows" was deleted, it has been substituted with "by profession of the evangelical counsels in the Church."

Line 15: "stronger and more lasting *bonds* . . ."

> **COMMENT: For the text, see Abbott-Gallagher, page 74, Number 44, line 15, where *firmiora et stabiliora vincula* is translated as "firmer and steadier bonds." Perhaps more fitting to the context would be: "stronger and more lasting bonds."**

Calling attention to this terminology in the text itself, as many fathers desire, is not necessary. "Sacred bonds," which in their own way are likened to vows, is an expression that is also clear for the Orientals and one that they can use.

21 — Page 156, line 3: One father suggests that *"believer in Christ"* (in Latin: *christefidelis*) should be used here in place of "Religious," because before profession one is not yet a Religious.

R — The text uses the normal manner of speaking and can stay as it is.

> **COMMENT: As can be seen from Qualification 20, Line 2, page 81, which was included in the final draft, the decision given in this reply was subsequently revoked.**

22 — Page 156, line 6: One father objects, saying that a Religious *in simple vows* retains ownership "of all (i.e., the goods) that he has."

R — There is no question here of a juridical norm, but of consecration.

> **COMMENT: In spite of this reply, the observation of the father was ultimately honored. The text, which originally read: "so totally to God . . . that he *and all that he has* become committed . . ." was changed to read as indicated in Qualification 20, Line 2.**

23 — Page 156, lines 11-12: One father wants the words "from . . . the perfection of divine worship" (in Latin: *a . . . divini cultus perfectione*) substituted by "the perfection *of the sacred liturgy,*" or by "the perfection *of divine offices,*" because the word *worship* ought to be avoided.

R — *"Worship"* was used intentionally with the adjective *"divine."*

> **COMMENT: For the text in question, see: Abbott-Gallagher, page 74, lines 7 and 8 from the bottom.**

24 — Page 156, line 13: One father states that the word "*to consecrate*" indicates divine action; for a human action one ought to say *devote* or *give oneself* to (in Latin: *devovere* or *mancipare*).

R — The new text will read: "*Through these same bonds he is* more intimately *consecrated* to divine service"; the construction is passive and the words "by God" are to be understood after "consecrated."

> **COMMENT: Compare Line 13 in Qualification 20. For some reason unknown to the author the words *"through these same bonds"* were not included in the list of acceptable qualifications which the Doctrinal Commission presented to the council fathers. The reason may well be that indicated in the final sentence of the COMMENT under Line 13 in Qualification 20.**

25 — Page 156, lines 14-17: Six fathers propose that these lines be deleted because they are ambiguous.

R — Greater perfection is affirmed *about the form of life,* not about the *individual* who observes it.

> **COMMENT: The translation of this important passage by Abbott-Gallagher, page 74,**

lines 3 to 6 from the bottom, is faulty. The
final Latin text reads: "The consecration,
however, will be so much the more perfect,
the more that Christ is represented—through
stronger and more lasting bonds—as being
joined by an indissoluble bond to His
spouse, the Church." The "stronger and
more lasting bonds" refer back to the
"vows" or "other sacred ties" mentioned in
Qualification 20, Line 2.

26 – Page 156, lines 14-17: After the words "more
intimately consecrated to divine service," 370 fathers
propose that there be added these words quoted from
the solemn Allocution of Paul VI to Religious of May
23, 1964: *The profession of the evangelical vows* (sic!)
*is therefore joined to the consecration which is proper to
Baptism, and like a peculiar kind of consecration it
brings this earlier one to completion, in so far as the
believer in Christ commits and devotes himself totally to
God, placing his whole life at the service of God alone."*

R – This has already been provided for in the replies
to Qualifications 2 and 16. After the words " . . . consecrated to divine service" (line 13) a reference to Footnote 2 is being inserted.

COMMENT: In Abbott-Gallagher, this is
footnote 213 on page 74.

27 – Page 156, lines 18-29: One father suggests a new
structure for the entire paragraph in order to obtain a
more logical sequence.

COMMENT: In Abbott-Gallagher the paragraph begins on page 74, two lines from the
bottom.

R – The sequence as given in the text can be retained.

28 — Page 156, lines 27-29: Two fathers propose that these lines be deleted (because the Church in fact has suppressed some Institutes), while another father suggests that the text read: "It is for this reason that in the Church the character proper to the various Institutes is *protected and fostered,*" lest the word *Church* be used only for the hierarchy.

R — The word *Church* means the *whole* Church, namely the pastors and the faithful.

> **COMMENT: In Abbott-Gallagher the text referred to is on page 75, lines 8-10. "Protects" would appear to be a better translation than "preserves," the word used by Abbott-Gallagher, because the final Latin text has:** *Unde et Ecclesia . . . tuetur . . .*

29 — Pages 156, line 31: One father proposes that after the words "The profession of the evangelical counsels," there should be added: "if it is really made sincerely."

R — This is self-evident.

> **COMMENT: Cf. Abbott-Gallagher, page 75, line 11.**

30 — Page 156, line 37: Three fathers suggest that "in a particular way" be used in place of "more adequately."

R — The text can remain as it is.

> **COMMENT: Cf. Abbott-Gallagher, page 75, line 17.**

31 — Page 156, line 36, and also page 157, line 12: Four fathers propose that instead of *"religious state"* one should say *"profession of the counsels."* Two others ask that on page 157 these words of lines 12-14 should be deleted because they are not clear: "Thus, although

the . . . to her life and holiness." Still another father proposes that in this same place one should say either: "although it does not belong to the hierarchical structure of the Church, *and is not the only way of reaching Christian perfection, nevertheless . . .,*" or: ". . .*nor is it to be considered the only way of reaching perfection,* nevertheless . . ."

> **COMMENT: Page 156, line 36, is equivalent to Abbott-Gallagher, page 75, line 16. Page 157, lines 12-14, are equivalent to lines 2 to 5 from the bottom of page 75 in Abbott-Gallagher.**

R — In the text the profession of the counsels is not proposed as the *only* way, but as a *particular* way. "The religious state" will be kept on page 156, line 36. And line 12 on page 157 will be made to read: "Therefore the state *which is constituted by the profession of the evangelical counsels . . ."*

> **COMMENT: Page 156, line 36, is line 16, page 75, in Abbott-Gallagher. Note that the word "religious" should be deleted from Abbott-Gallagher, page 75, line 5 from the bottom.**

32 — Page 157, line 7: One father proposes that after "reveals" *there be added: "in its own way."*

R — The text will be made to read: *"in a unique way."*

> **COMMENT: Cf. Abbott-Gallagher, page 75, line 11 from the bottom.**

33 — Page 157, line 14: One father proposes that the word *"inseparably" be deleted*, because the assertion is theologically and historically false.

R — The affirmation *about the profession of the counsels,* which constitutes a recognized state in the

Church, can certainly stay.

> **COMMENT: In the draft under scrutiny the affirmation was made about "the religious state," which was altered as explained in Qualification 31 to: "the profession of the evangelical counsels." See also the COMMENT to the Reply under that same Qualification.**

Number 45

34 – Page 157, lines 15-16: One father proposes that in the title, in place of "Under the authority of the Church," the text should read: "Under the authority of the Hierarchy," so as not to use the word "Church" for the hierarchy alone.

R – There is no possible equivocation.

> **COMMENT: On the significance of these titles for the various Numbers, see page 6 of this book.**

35 – Page 157, lines 18-22: Five fathers propose that the text: "it devolves on the same hierarchy to govern ... the evangelical counsels and the profession of them," should be changed to read: "it devolves on the same hierarchy to govern with wise legislation the *practice and profession* of the evangelical counsels reinforced by vows." For authority does not govern the counsels themselves, but their practice.

R – Let the other words of the original text remain as they are, but write "*practice of the* evangelical counsels."

> **COMMENT: For the passage, see Abbott-Gallagher, page 76, lines 2-5.**

36 – Page 157, line 21: One father proposes that in place of "also confirmed by vows," one should use "also

confirmed by vows *or any other form.*"

R — The addition is useless.

> **COMMENT: The laconic reply must mean
> that the *entire* phrase was useless: "also con-
> firmed by vows or any other form," because
> none of it appears in the finally adopted
> text. See also Abbott-Gallagher, page 76,
> lines 2-5. The words "also confirmed by
> vows" were missing in the second draft, were
> inserted in the third draft, and were left out
> of the fourth draft. Perhaps this addition
> was called "useless" in view of Qualification
> 20, Line 2, page 81.**

37 — Page 157, lines 23-26: One father proposes that
the following words be deleted: "Submissively following
. . . authentically approves later modifications," because
they suggest that the Church is infallible in reviewing
rules.

R — There is no talk of infallibility. Therefore let the
text stand.

> **COMMENT: For the text in question see:
> Abbott-Gallagher, page 76 lines 6-8.**

38 — Page 157, lines 26-28: One father proposes that
after the words: "approves later modifications," there be
added: "*by adapting them to the life of the Church as
time goes on.*" Another father asks that for the expression: "*in every way*," these words should be substituted: "*always faithful to the germane spirit of the founders.*"

R — The first petition is provided for in the schema
on Religious. As for the second, the text will be drafted
to read: "so that they can grow and flourish *in accord
with the spirit of their founders.*"

> **COMMENT: For the passage, see: Abbott-Gallagher, page 76, lines 9-12.**

39 — Page 157, line 29: One father asks that something be added for fostering vocations to the religious state.

R — This question does not pertain to a dogmatic exposition.

> **COMMENT: The request was that the addition be made immediately after line 12 on page 76 in Abbott-Gallagher.**

40 — Page 157, line 30, to page 158, line 3: All of these Qualifications deal with the exemption of Religious.

The *first* series is of a *general nature*. One father suggests that the entire section should be deleted; another father suggests that at least a notable part of it be deleted (lines 30-38); and finally a third father proposes a new revision of the entire paragraph, lest the significance of exemption be stressed too much.

On the other hand, 373 fathers insisting on the meaningfulness of exemption, propose an addition of 12 lines taken from the Allocution of His Holiness Paul VI to Religious (23 May 1964).

> **COMMENT: For line 30, page 157, to line 3, page 158, see Abbott-Gallagher, page 76, the entire paragraph which begins: "Any institute of perfection . . ." For lines 30-38, see** *ibid.,* **the first nine lines of the same paragraph.**

The *second* series deals *with particulars*. Three fathers propose changes for lines 33-36: Instead of saying: "can be . . . subjected to him alone . . . by virtue of his primacy over the entire Church," the text should read: "can be . . . subjected to *himself* . . . by virtue of his primacy *of jurisdiction* over the entire Church." Another father thinks the words: "can be removed from the jurisdiction of the local Ordinaries" *ought to be deleted*, whereas another asks for the *suppression* of the phrase: " in consideration of the common good." Still another proposes a *new* text for the lines 30-36: "Any institute of perfection . . . the common good."

Finally, three fathers take another direction. The first proposes that in place of "to him alone" in line 35, the text should read: " to him *and to the college of Bishops.*" The second asks that in line 37, after the words "patriarchal authorities," *there should be added: "or the territorial conferences of Bishops."* The third, finally, asks that in line 36, after: "can be . . . subjected to him alone," *there be added: "The Supreme Pontiff, however, for pastoral reasons and for the benefit of souls can transfer this jurisdiction to the Local Ordinary."*

> **COMMENT: The page and line references are to the same paragraph mentioned in the previous COMMENT.**

R – To the *first* series: The proposals do not conform with the general norms. Further, the text already approved is general and has been drawn up prudently and without any polemical intentions. As for including the Allocution of His Holiness Paul VI, provision for this has already been made earlier in the text; here a reference to it will be added in Footnote 6.

> **COMMENT: Footnote 6 became footnote 219 in Abbott-Gallagher on page 76. The Latin text referred to by the footnote reference reads:**

> **"The exemption of religious orders is in no**

way repugnant to the divinely established constitution of the Church. By reason of this constitution every priest, especially as regards his functions in the sacred ministry, must obey the hierarchy. Now the members of a religious community are always and everywhere subject primarily to the power of the Roman Pontiff, since he as it were is their highest superior. Religious institutes therefore are at the service of the Roman Pontiff for those works which are for the benefit of the universal Church. As for activities connected with the sacred apostolate in the various dioceses, however, the members of religious communities are also subject to the jurisdiction of bishops—whom they are obliged to help—under the condition that the nature of the apostolate that is characteristically theirs be preserved, and under the condition that the needs of the religious life be provided for. It is evident from this how much the Church benefits when Religious give their collaboration and assistance to the diocesan clergy, since forces that are united become stronger and more effective."

In view of this quotation of the Pope, in view of the official commentary of the Doctrinal Commission on exemption, and in view of the efforts made in the preparatory phase of Vatican II by some bishops to have exemption abolished, it would appear that the primary purpose of the teaching contained in Number 45 was to affirm and confirm such exemption. The emphasis placed on another purpose by the Rev. Avery Dulles, S.J., in Abbott-Gallagher, page 76, footnote 217, namely, "to correct the impression that papal exemption withdraws the members of an exempt order from obedience to the hierarchy," hardly seems warranted. Like all other footnotes in Abbott-Gallagher not printed in italics, this one does not occur in the Constitution on the Church as approved by the council fathers.

To the *second* series: The reference to the primacy suffices as it stands. Line 33, however, will read: "by reason of the primacy *itself* over the universal Church." The other ideas that have been proposed are already mentioned, as regards their essentials, in the text as approved; or they pertain to juridical particulars which ought not be taken up here.

COMMENT: The Abbott-Gallagher translation on page 76, line 4, in the paragraph: "Any institute of perfection . . .," speaks of *"his* primacy." The finally approved text reads: "by reason of the primacy *itself* over the universal Church." (In Latin: *ratione ipsius in universam Ecclesiam primatus.)*

41 – Page 157, lines 38-41: These qualifications deal rather with the relationship between Bishops and "exempt" Religious. One father proposes that after: "committed to the charge of their proper patriarchal authorities," this *should be added: "But since there is no admittance to the universal Church except through the local Church, let them recognize that they have a role in the local Church and that they constitute this community's animating principle."* Three others propose that after "obedience" in line 40 *there should be added: "like diocesan priests, promptly and faithfully,* as required by canonical laws." Another father *adds: "and the greatest cooperation (omitting*: as required by canonical laws)" and also "pastoral authority *that ought*

to be recognized."

There are still two other fathers who wish to have *omitted* the words: *"as required by canonical laws,"* whereas one father suggests that after the words "Bishops . . . by canonical laws" in lines 40-41, there *should be added: "and they are subject to the Local Ordinary in everything that concerns apostolic activity* because of *his* pastoral authority over an *individual* Church, and because of necessary unity in apostolic labor" (omitting therefore on page 158, line 3: *"and harmony"*).

> **COMMENT:** For lines 38-41, see Abbott-Gallagher, page 76, lines 5-10 from the bottom.

R – *The additions* are not opportune, because these ideas have already been sufficiently provided for in the text. On the other hand, the insertion *"as required by canonical laws"* is necessary. Similarly the notion *of harmony* is required. The text can therefore remain as it is.

42 – Page 158, lines 4-9: One father objects to the word *"Church"* in the sense of hierarchy, to the words *"religious* profession" since "religious" is too restrictive, to the words "a state *consecrated* to God" because "consecrated" is used in a rather broad sense, and to the word *"manifests"* because religious profession, according to the Constitution on the Sacred Liturgy, is "sacramental." He proposes the following amended text: *"In* the Church, however, the profession *of the counsels* is not only *raised* to the dignity of a canonical state by juridical sanction, but also by a liturgical act *is elevated to* a state consecrated to God. For the Church herself, *through her lawful ministers,* accepts the vows of those professing them." Three fathers propose another version: ". . . but also by its liturgical act

makes it like a state consecrated *by* God."

R — As for the use of the words, this has already been taken care of above. The word *"manifests"* can by all means be used in reference to some sacramental. The slight additions are not necessary. Therefore the text can stand.

> **COMMENT: In Abbott-Gallagher the text referred to is in the last four lines on page 76 and the first two lines on page 77.**

43 — Page 158, lines 6-7: One father requests that in a footnote it be said "that the exemplariness of the religious life ought to be stated in an *assertive* and not in an exclusive way."

> **COMMENT: The text in Abbott-Gallagher is on page 76, the last four lines.**

R — Provision for this has already been made earlier. See Qualification 19.

Number 46

44 — Page 158, line 15: One father thinks that an amended *title* ought to be proposed as follows: *"Profession of the evangelical counsels* ought to be appreciated"*, because of reasons already explained on an earlier occasion.

> **COMMENT: The provisional title at this time at the head of Number 46 was: "Consecration through the evangelical counsels ought to be appreciated."**

R — The proposal is accepted.

45 — Page 158, line 16 (and line 40): One father proposes that in place of the word "Religious" a more general term should be used, namely, *"those who profess*

the counsels," because of the reasons already offered in Qualification 20.

> **COMMENT: For these passages see: Abbott-Gallagher, page 77, Number 46, the first line of the first and third paragraphs.**

R — This has already been provided for in Qualification 20 and elsewhere.

46 — Page 158, lines 35-36: Three fathers suggest that in place of "especially . . . with the kind of virginal and poor life," one should write: "especially . . . with the kind of virginal, poor *and obedient* life," because in the religious life "obedience is a more perfect and more complete holocaust of one's person."

> **COMMENT: In Abbott-Gallagher the text referred to is on page 77, Number 46, second paragraph, in the second and third lines from the end. The Abbott-Gallagher translation is faulty here; suggested in its place is the translation given in the COMMENT on page 43 of this book.**

R — Obedience does not determine a special kind of life.

47 — Page 159, line 10: One father proposes that after the words "or in schools" *there should be added: "or in social institutes"*; another father proposes the following *addition: " . . .who both in the homeland and in the missions, in schools and in hospitals, in their religious houses and in the world, or by any other kind of activity,* adorn the Bride of Christ."

> **COMMENT: For this passage see: Abbott-Gallagher, page 78, lines 1 to 4.**

R — Everything cannot be listed. What is listed is to be understood *by way of example,* and not in an exclusive sense. Besides, the proposals indicate different *places* rather than different *activities.*

48 — Page 159, line 12: Because he is not satisfied with the words: "by their faithful and humble *practice of the consecration* mentioned above," one father proposes that the text should read: *"by their unswerving and humble loyalty to the above-mentioned consecration."*

R — The proposal is accepted.

> **COMMENT: Abbott-Gallagher, page 78, lines 4-5, has changed "the above-mentioned consecration," found in the final text, to "their chosen consecration."**

Number 47

49 — Page 159, lines 15-22: Six fathers mention that this paragraph is a conclusion rather for Chapter V, *"The Call to Holiness,"* than for Chapter VI, *"Religious."* Three fathers propose drafting the text like this: *"Let each Religious* be diligent, *therefore,* in taking care *to remain to the end in the particular vocation that he has received from God, and let him busy himself with reaching excellence in it through the constant and perfect observance of the constitutions and rules of his institute. For this is the only right and sure path for Religious to follow in fulfilling the divine will, if they are to manifest* a type of holiness in the Church that is more fruitful, and if they are to promote the greater glory of the one and undivided Trinity, which in Christ and through Christ is the fountain and the wellspring of all the holiness *of men."*

COMMENT: The paragraph being criticized began: "Let each one of the faithful be diligent, therefore, in taking care to remain to the end in the vocation—whatever it may be—to which he has been called by God . . ."

R — *The amplification* is not necessary. Line 16 will be changed to read: "Let each one, however, *who has been called to the profession of the counsels*, be diligent in taking care to remain to the end in that vocation to *which* he has been called by God."

COMMENT: Abbott-Gallagher, page 78, Number 47, contains some ideas not in the final Latin text, namely: "all," "vows," "their purpose," "more vigorous flowering," etc. In Abbott-Gallagher all subjects are in the plural: in Latin all subjects and verbs are in the singular. A translation closer to the original would be:

"Let each one, however, who has been called to the profession of the counsels, be diligent in taking care to remain to the end in that vocation to which he has been called by God, and also to keep excelling in it. As a result, the holiness of the Church will become more fruitful, and there will be greater glory for the one and undivided Trinity, that in Christ and through Christ is the fountain and origin of all holiness."

50 — Page 159, line 18: One father makes the observation that the words: *"to remain to the end in the vocation—whatever it may be—to which he has been called by God."* are perhaps too absolute.

R — The affirmation as contained in the text is general.

COMMENT: As is evident from Qualification 49, the words "whatever it may be" have been altered in the final text.

Chapter Eight

QUALIFICATIONS AND REPLIES: ON HOLINESS

Chapter Eight

QUALIFICATIONS AND REPLIES: ON HOLINESS[14]

COMMENT: Early in the third session, on September 30, 1964, the council fathers were asked if they were satisfied with the third draft of Chapter V on Holiness (Paragraph Numbers 39-42). The voting returns were:

Yes:	1856
Yes (with qualifications):	302
No:	17
Void:	2
Total:	2177

This meant that the chapter as a whole, together with each of its parts, was approved by the general assembly.

As in the case of the chapter on Religious, a booklet containing all qualifications and replies was then prepared by the Doctrinal Commission and on November 14 (together with the one on Religious) was distributed to the council fathers. Of the 41 headings under which the qualifications were grouped, only the first heading—which was also the longest one—was devoted to general qualifications. All the rest dealt with specific points. Since the general qualifications of the chapter on holiness were intimately connected with the chapter on Religious, they and the replies to them fall within the scope

---

[14] The source as cited in footnote 11, pp. 17-18.

of the present work, and so will be given here. They were preceded by an introductory paragraph.

All of the qualifications submitted by the fathers have been diligently examined by the Most Excellent F. Seper, president of the subcommission in charge of this chapter, and also by the secretaries of the Doctrinal Commission, together with the Most Excellent Charue who was delegated as president of this technical commission by the president of the Doctrinal Commission.

In General

1 — Three qualifications of a general nature have been submitted. Some fathers ask that *the single chapter* be retained and they proposed a new sequence for the material. On the other hand there are 584 fathers who ask that the entire chapter should be relocated after Chapter II on the *People of God.* Finally, there is one father who asks that a new revision should make it appear more clearly *that Christ is the exemplar* and the source of holiness for all; he also asks—and here he is joined by another father—that mention should be made of the higher degrees in the life of grace.

R — *The first* proposal contradicts the decision of the general assembly. Although reasons which must not be rejected are offered for *the second* proposal, the proposal itself cannot be carried out, and this because of a decision of the general assembly and also because of practical reasons, especially the urgent time factor. The proposals in *the third* qualification have already been provided for sufficiently in the text: compare, for example, page 139, lines 5 ff. As for the higher degrees in the life of grace, however, this is not to be treated here.

> **COMMENT**: The page and line references
> mentioned begin in Abbott-Gallagher on
> page 66, line 1.

Although strictly speaking the *wishes* (in Latin: *votum*) submitted on September 15, 1964, by 584 council fathers are not a "qualification," because "those who voted with qualifications" on September 30 were only 302, nevertheless the technical subcommission used all due care in examining their document and the reasons presented in it.

1) After the complete approbation of Chapter II on the *People of God* and its amendments by the general assembly on October 30, 1964, it is no longer allowed to introduce *changes* in it.

2) As for *transferring* Chapter V (on Holiness) to a position immediately after Chapter II, this has already been discussed above. As regards the reasons on which the request was based, however, the Doctrinal Commission would like to make the following observations, so that we may do our best to satisfy those who presented the request.

a) That *absolutely all* in the Church are called to holiness is stated *explicitly* in the introduction of this Chapter V, namely, on page 139, lines 10-14; and then this is taught avowedly in Number 40: "On *the universal* call to holiness." This vocation, therefore, cannot appear as if it were reserved to Religious.

> **COMMENT**: "The universal call to holiness"
> was the title of Number 40 in Chapter V of
> the third draft. In the same draft this title
> was also part of the chapter title itself: "The
> Universal Call to Holiness in the Church,"
> and this remained the title of the chapter in

the final draft. Abbott-Gallagher on page 65 phrased the Latin this way: "The Call of the Whole Church to Holiness." The Latin reads: *De universali vocatione ad sanctitatem in Ecclesia.*

b) As for *the state of Religious in the Church:* in view of the importance of this state, it is being treated in a special and distinct Chapter, namely VI.

c) Although *the sequence of the chapters,* as they now stand, is not perfect in every respect, it is nevertheless justified by the considerations presented in the report, page 178, f., where pontifical documents are also quoted.

COMMENT: The section of the report here referred to is discussed in Chapter 5 of this book, CONCLUSION, starting with "3)" and going to the end of the chapter (see pages 60-63).

In Particular

3) As for what concerns *particulars*—among other things the *ecclesiological* aspect of Religious—we have diligently taken care of this, as will become still more clearly evident from the present report on what was done about the qualifications.

4) *The Declarations of His Holiness Paul VI* of May 23, 1964, on the perennial value of the religious life, on the renewal to be brought about prudently in it, on the relationship between the interior life and the apostolate, and on concord with the sacred hierarchy, are honored and used with diligence at various places in the text. The insertion in the text of longer quotations, however, is not in accordance with the general norms. Those *Decla-*

rations are therefore referred to accurately in the foot-notes.

COMMENT: With these remarks the reply to the general qualifications ended. The reader might well be interested, however, in learning a bit more about the discrepancy between the figures 302 and 584 in the first paragraph above ("Although strictly . . .") on page 105.

Chronology

In January, 1964, between the second and third Sessions of Vatican II, some members of the joint subcommission strongly opposed the position taken by the commission on Religious, the Bishops Secretariat, and the majority of the superiors general regarding how or what emphasis was to be placed on the religious life, and especially on where in the Church schema the teaching on the universal vocation to holiness should be located.

The Doctrinal Commission in March in plenary session also refused to accede to the wishes of the three groups.

Religious then won the sympathy of Pope Paul VI for their cause; because on May 23 in his Allocution to Religious called *Magno gaudio* (i.e., *With great joy*) he gave his support to many teachings strongly contested by some members of the Doctrinal Commission but earnestly requested by the commission on Religious, the Bishops Secretariat, and the majority of superiors general. The "Religious" to whom the Allocution was addressed were the superiors general of several religious communities having their general chapters in Rome, and also the chapter delegates.

On July 22 the Bishops Secretariat mailed

a letter to hundreds of council fathers around the world, asking for their signatures in support of a list of enclosed *Wishes.* Also accompanying the letter was a translation in each bishop's vernacular from the Latin of Pope Paul's Allocution of May 23 to Religious.

The result was that 584 council fathers sent in their signatures for the *Wishes* to the Bishops Secretariat which then handed them over to the Doctrinal Commission on September 15, 1964, the day after the solemn opening of the third session.

Some bishops, however, needed a second letter as a reminder, and this was sent to them immediately after they arrived in Rome for the third session. This resulted in an additional 224 signatures, which also were given by the Bishops Secretariat to the Doctrinal Commission. This brought the total to 808 signatures and included those of 82 superiors general. The names of all the signatories were noted in the records of the Bishops Secretariat.

When the vote was taken on September 30 on the suitability and content of the Chapter on Holiness (its location, etc.), the 808 council fathers did not consider it necessary to present *again* as qualifications what they had already formally presented to the Doctrinal Commission in the two preceding weeks. As a result there were no more than 302 council fathers who submitted affirmative votes *with qualifications.* On the basis of the 302 vote, the Doctrinal Commission argued that it had received for the chapter on Holiness from the council fathers the necessary two-thirds majority, since 1856 or 85 per cent of the 2177 council fathers had submitted unqualified votes. Had the mind of the 808 council fathers been considered as "qualified affirmative votes," then the Doctrinal Commission would have received a maximum of 1350 unqualified affirmative votes or only 62 per cent. It would have then been obliged to revise the text according to the *Wishes* of the 808 in order to gain the necessary two-thirds majority.

When the 808 council fathers on November 14 received the explanation from the Doctrinal Commission on what it had done with their *Wishes*, as indicated earlier in this present chapter, there was surprise and disappointment.

One alternative would have been for the 808 to cast a negative vote on November 17, when they were asked if they were satisfied with the way the qualifications for the chapter on Holiness had been handled. Since 2146 council fathers actually voted that day, this would have resulted in only a 62 per cent affirmative vote at the very highest. In other words, the fourth draft would have been rejected and the Doctrinal Commission would have had to prepare a fifth draft, honoring the *Wishes* of the 808. Thus it would have been impossible for the Dogmatic Constitution on the Church to be promulgated at the end of the third session.

The Bishops Secretariat, which originally had called for the support of the 808, pondered the matter and decided that it had already gained much. At the same time it feared that all of this might be jeopardized by a negative vote at this stage. And so, even though some considered the action of the Doctrinal Commission in this case as "scandalous," the Bishops Secretariat let it be known that it seemed best to cast an affirmative vote on the Doctrinal Commission's handling of the qualifications for the Chapter on Holiness.

Chapter Nine

THE GENERAL ASSEMBLY VOTES AGAIN

Chapter Nine

THE GENERAL ASSEMBLY
VOTES AGAIN

COMMENT: The council fathers were asked on November 17, 1964, to vote on whether or not they were pleased with the way in which the Doctrinal Commission had replied to the qualifications on Chapter V on Holiness, and with the corrections that the commission had decided to incorporate in the text. They voted as follows:

Yes:	2142
No:	4
Total:	2146[15]

On the next day, November 18, they were asked the same questions about chapter VI on Religious. On the basis of the 50 qualifications listed in chapter 7 of this present work, the Doctrinal Commission introduced 11 corrections for the text and listed these at the end of its booklet on qualifications, spelling them out in detail. They were the same as those indicated in the replies to qualifications 11, 15, 20, 31, 32, 35, 38, 40, 44, 48 and 49, and so they need not be repeated here. Once again the council fathers approved the work of the Doctrinal Commission. The vote was:

Yes:	2114
No:	12
Void:	5
Total:	2131

---

[15] All voting returns listed in this chapter are from Giovanni Caprile, S.J., **II Concilio Vaticano II: Terzo Periodo 1964-65**, Vol. IV (Edizioni "La Civilta Cattolica," Rome, 1965), p. 365.

Then two days before the closing of the third session, on November 19, the schema on the Church as a whole, and as revised by the corrections already accepted through individual ballots for each chapter, was voted upon. In this semi-final vote the council fathers were asked if they were pleased with the text as revised, now in its fourth draft. The results of the voting were these:

Yes:	2134
No:	10
Void:	1
Total:	2145

The definitive vote took place on November 21, the last day of the third session, at a public session and in the presence of the Pope. For the last time the council fathers were asked if they were pleased with the Dogmatic Constitution on the Church, and with all of its parts. They then voted as follows:

Yes:	2151
No:	5
Total:	2156

After Pope Paul was privately informed of the voting returns, they were announced publicly and there was sustained applause. Only a two-thirds majority was required for passage, but for all practical purposes the vote was unanimous, since 99-3/4 per cent of the council fathers had voted "Yes."

Pope Paul then promulgated the Dogmatic Constitution on the Church, and once again there was loud applause.

Chapter Ten

APPENDIX
LATIN TEXT OF CHAPTER VI
SCHEMA REVISION OF
JULY 3, 1964

NOTE: The *Textus prior* (second draft) and the *Textus emendatus* (third draft) were printed in parallel columns, so that the council fathers could see at a glance what alterations had been made. The changes in the new draft were indicated by italics.

The letters (A), (B), etc., refer to corresponding letters in the commentary on pages 31-46 of this book. The equivalent lettering for Abbott-Gallagher is indicated on page 5.

The numbers (1), (2), etc., refer to the footnotes on pages 130f.

The page references in the qualifications on Religious (see pages 73-99 of this book) refer to the page numbering of the Latin text reprinted here.

R.M.W.

CAPUT VI
(SIVE: CAP. V, SECTIO B)
DE RELIGIOSIS

1	32. *(De praxi consiliorum in statu vitae*
2	*ab Ecclesia sancito).* Ad consilia evangelica,
3	in verbis et exemplis Domini fundata, ab Apo-
4	stolis et Patribus, Ecclesiaeque doctoribus et
5	pastoribus commendata, plures christiani vocati
6	accedunt, immo praxim eorum instituunt in
7	stabili vivendi forma, ab Ecclesia sancita, quae
8	status perfectionis acquirendae vocatur. Quae
9	institutio, velut arbor ex germine divinitus da-
10	to mirabiliter et multipliciter in agro Domini
11	crescit et ramis diffunditur.
12	
13	
14	
15	
16	
17	
18	
19	
20	
21	
22	
23	
24	

CAPUT VI
(SIVE: CAP. V, SECTIO B)
DE RELIGIOSIS

1   43. (olim n. 32). *(De professione Consilio-*
2 *rum evangelicorum in Ecclesia). Consilia evan-*
3 *gelica (A) castitatis Deo dicatae, paupertatis et*
4 *oboedientiae,* utpote in verbis et exemplis Do-
5 mini fundata et ab Apostolis et Patribus Ec-
6 clesiaeque doctoribus et pastoribus commen-
7 data, *sunt donum divinum, quod Ecclesia a*
8 *Domino suo accepit et gratia Eius semper con-*
9 *servat. Ad ipsam quoque pertinet illa interpre-*
10 *tari, eorum praxim moderari et etiam stabiles*
11 *inde vivendi formas constituere.* Quo factum
12 est (B) ut, quasi in arbore ex germine divinitus
13 dato mirabiliter et multipliciter in agro Do-
14 mini ramificata, *variae formae vitae solitariae*
15 *vel communis, variaeque familiae creverint,*
16 *quae tum ad profectum sodalium, tum ad bo-*
17 *num totius Corporis Christi opes augent (1).*
18 *Illae enim familiae sodalibus suis adminicula*
19 *conferunt* stabilitatis in modo vivendi firmio-
20 ris, *doctrinae ad perfectionem prosequendam*
21 *probatae, communionis in militia Christi fra-*
22 *ternae, libertatis per oboedientiam amplificatae,*
23 *ita ut suam religiosam professionem secure*
24 *implere et fideliter custodire valeant, atque*

117

[Textus prior, p. 155 cont'd]

25
26   Status huiusmodi, ratione habita divinae
27   Ecclesiae constitutionis, non est intermedium
28   quid inter clericalem et laicalem condicionem,
29   sed ex utraque parte christifideles quidam a
30   Deo vocantur, ut in Ecclesiae mysterio pecu-
31   liari dono fruantur et servitio mancipentur.
32

[Textus prior, p. 156]

1   33. *(De momento statuum perfectionis ac-*
2   *quirendae in Ecclesia).* Cum Christus sua vi-
3   vendi forma exemplar sit omnium virtutum,
4   ideo in Ecclesia, in qua mysterium Eius indesi-
5   nenter viget et operatur, numquam deerunt
6   qui consilia evangelica expresse profitebuntur.
7   In Ecclesia enim plenior illa abnegatio, quae
8   in horum consiliorum professione continetur,
9   dum Christi exinanitionem et crucem pressius
10   imitatur, novam vitam redemptione Christi ac-
11   quisitam manifestius per proprium statum si-
12   gnificat et resurrectionem et gloriam regni cae-
13   lestis clarius praenuntiat.
14   Consiliorum professio est in Ecclesia Spi-
15   ritus Sancti fructus pretiosus, eiusque sancti-
16   tatis peculiare testimonium, cum via praeclara
17   sit amoris indivisi erga Deum (cf. 1 Cor. 7,
18   31-34), quo christifideles non solum interius
19   sed exteriore quoque vitae ratione soli Chri-
20   sto adhaerent.

25   *in caritatis via spiritu gaudentes progrediantur.*
26   Status huiusmodi (C), ratione habita divi-
27   nae *et hierarchicae* Ecclesiae constitutionis, non
28   est intermedius inter clericalem et laicalem
29   conditionem, sed ex utraque parte quidam
30   christifideles a Deo vocantur, ut in *vita* Eccle-
31   siae peculiari dono fruantur et, *suo quisque*
32   *modo, eiusdem missioni salvificae prosint (2).*

[Textus emendatus, p. 156]

1   44. (olim n. 33). *(De natura et momento*
2   *status religiosi in Ecclesia) (A). Per vota, qui-*
3   *bus religiosus ad tria praedicta consilia evan-*
4   *gelica se obligat (B), Deo summe dilecto tota-*
5   *liter mancipatur, ita ut ipse omniaque sua ad*
6   *Dei servitium Eiusque honorem novo et pecu-*
7   *liari titulo referantur. Per baptismum quidem*
8   *mortuus est peccato, et Deo sacratus; ut autem*
9   *gratiae baptismalis uberiorem fructum perci-*
10 *pere queat, votis liberari intendit ab impedi-*
11 *mentis, quae ipsum a caritatis fervore et di-*
12 *vini cultus perfectione retrahere possent, et*
13 *iisdem votis divino obsequio intimius consecra-*
14 *tur. Tanto autem perfectior erit consecratio,*
15 *quo per firmiora et stabiliora vota magis reprae-*
16 *sentatur Christus cum sponsa Ecclesia indis-*
17 *solubili vinculo coniunctus.*
18   Cum vero evangelica consilia (C) suos as-
19 seclas, per caritatem ad quam ducunt (3), Ec-
20 clesiae eiusque mysterio speciali modo coniun-

LATIN TEXT

[Textus prior, p. 156 cont'd]

21   Ideo cum evangelica consilia suos asseclas,
22 per caritatem ad quam ducunt, Ecclesiae eius-
23 que mysterio speciali modo coniungant, spiri-
24 tualis horum vita bono totius Ecclesiae devo-
25 veatur oportet. Propterea consiliorum profes-
26 sio illos, quos Deus vocavit, praecelse adiuvat,
27 ut sive prece, sive etiam actuosa opera, vitam
28 Salvatoris, perenniter in Ecclesia praesentis, in
29 se clarius exprimant. Cum enim a Dei dilectio-
30 ne defluat ipse proximi amor, a professione
31 sanctitatem sectandi derivat officium, cum ea
32 intime connexum, pro viribus scilicet prece
33 actuosaque opera laborandi ad regnum Chri-
34 sti in animis radicandum et roborandum, illud-
35 que ad omnes plagas dilatandum.
36
37
38
39
40
41
42

[Textus prior, p. 157]

1
2
3
4
5
6
7

21 gant, spiritualis horum vita bono quoque totius
22 Ecclesiae devoveatur oportet. Inde oritur of-
23 ficium pro viribus *et secundum forman pro-*
24 *priae vocationis,* sive oratione, sive actuosa
25 quoque opera, laborandi ad Regnum Christi
26 in animis radicandum et roborandum, illudque
27 ad omnes plagas dilatandum. *Unde et Ecclesia*
28 *propriam indolem variorum Institutorum re-*
29 *ligiosorum tuetur et fovet.*
30   *Evangelicorum proinde consiliorum pro-*
31 *fessio (D) tamquam signum apparet, quod om-*
32 *nia Ecclesiae membra ad officia vocationis chri-*
33 *stianae impigre adimplenda efficaciter attrahere*
34 *potest ac debet. Cum enim Populus Dei hic ma-*
35 *nentem civitatem non habeat, sed futuram in-*
36 *quirat, status religiosus, qui suos assectas a cu-*
37 *ris terrenis magis liberat, magis etiam tum bo-*
38 *na coelestia iam in hoc saeculo prasentia om-*
39 *nibus credentibus manifestat, tum vitam novam*
40 *et aeternam redemptione Christi acquisitam*
41 *testificat, tum resurrectionem futuram et glo-*
42 *riam Regni coelestis praenuntiat. Forman quo-*

1 *que vitae, quam Filius Dei accepit, mundum*
2 *ingressus ut faceret voluntatem Patris, quam-*
3 *que discipulis Ipsum sequentibus proposuit,*
4 *idem status pressius imitatur atque in Ecclesia*
5 *perpetuo repraesentat. Regni Dei denique su-*
6 *per omnia terrestria elevationem eiusque sum-*
7 *mas necessitudines patefacit; supereminentem*

[Textus prior, p. 157 cont'd]

8
9
10
11
12
13
14
15   34. *(Sub auctoritate Ecclesiae)*. Cum ec-
16 clesiasticae auctoritatis munus sit populum Dei
17 pascere et ad pascua uberrima ducere (cf. Ez.
18 34, 14), ad ipsam pertinet evangelica consilia,
19 quibus perfectio caritatis erga Deum et proxi-
20 mum singulariter fovetur, fideliter explicare,
21 eorumque publicam professionem legibus suis
22 sapienter moderari, sicut inde ab antiquitate
23 pro coenobiis et monasteris provide fecit. Qua-
24 re Ecclesia, Spiritus Sancti impulsus docilis
25 sequens, Regulas a praeclaris viris et mulieri-
26 bus propositas cum laude recepit, et ulterius
27 ordinatas authentice adprobavit; necnon Insti-
28 tutis ad perfectionem prosequendam passim
29 erectis, ut omni modo crescant atque floreant,
30 auctoritate sua invigilante et protegente, sem-
31 per et ubique adfuit.
32   Quo autem melius necessitatibus totius
33 dominici gregis provideatur, Romanus Ponti-
34 fex, ratione sui in universam Ecclesiam prima-
35 tus, quodcumque perfectionis Institutum ac
36 sodales singulos, intuitu utiliatis communis,
37 sibi soli subiicere atque ab Ordinarii loci iuris-
38 dictione eximere potest. Quod attinet ad ipsos
39 sodales, iidem in officio erga Ecclesiam ex pe-

8   *quoque magnitudinem virtutis Christi regnan-*
9   *tis atque infinitam Spiritus Sancti potentiam,*
10   *in Ecclesia mirabiliter operantem, cunctis ho-*
11   *minibus demonstrat.*

12   *Status ergo religiosus (E), licet ad Ecclesiae*
13   *structuram hierarchicam non spectet, ad eius*
14   *tamen vitam et sanctitatem inconcusse pertinet.*

15   45. (olim n. 34). *(Sub auctoritate Eccle-*
16   *siae).* Cum ecclesiasticae Hierarchiae munus
17   sit (A) Populum Dei pascere et ad pascua uber-
18   rima ducere (cf. Ezech. 34, 14), ad ipsam
19   spectat evangelica consilia, quibus perfectio ca-
20   ritatis erga Deum et proximum singulariter fo-
21   vetur, eorumque professionem, *etiam votis fir-*
22   *matam,* legibus suis sapienter moderari (4).
23   Ipsa etiam, Spiritus Sancti impulsus dociliter
24   sequens, regulas a praeclaris viris et mulieribus
25   propositas recipit et ulterius ordinatas authen-
26   tice adprobat, necnon Institutis *ad aedificatio-*
27   *nem Corporis Christi* passim erectis, ut omni
28   modo crescant atque floreant, auctoritate sua
29   invigilante et protegente adest.

30   Quo autem melius (B) necessitatibus totius
31   dominici gregis provideatur, quodcumque per-
32   fectionis Institutum ac sodales singuli a *Summo*
33   *mo* Pontifice, ratione sui in universam Ecclesiam
34   primatus, intuitu utilitatis communis, ab Or-
35   dinariorum loci iurisdictione eximi et ei soli
36   subiici possunt (5). *Similiter possunt propriis*
37   *auctoritatibus patriarchalibus relinqui aut com-*
38   *mitti.* Ipsi sodales, in officio erga Ecclesiam
39   ex peculiari suae vitae forma adimplendo, reve-

123

LATIN TEXT

[Textus prior, p. 157 cont'd]

40   culiari suae vitae forma adimplendo, reveren-
41   tiam et oboedientiam, iuxta canonicas leges,

[Textus prior, p. 158]

1   prastare debent Episcopis, ob eorum in Eccle-
2   siis particularibus auctoritatem pastoralem et
3   ob necessariam in labore apostolico unitatem
4   et concordiam. Peculiari enim vocatione sua
5   constituti sunt validi et propinqui Sacrae Hie-
6   rarchiae ac ministrorum cooperatores necnon
7   fidelium adiutores in Regno Christi provehendo
8   et stabiliendo. Exemplis autem et laboribus suis
9   omnia Ecclesiae membra ad legem caritatis
10   impigre sectandam efficaciter attrahere possunt
11   ac debent.
12
13
14   35. *(Aestimanda est consecratio consilio-*
15   *rum evangelicorum).* Eo pluris evangelicorum
16   consiliorum professio per se aestimanda est,
17   quo intimior atque firmior fit Deo consecratio.
18   In singulis autem huius consecrationis meritum
19   a caritate qua imperatur maxime pendet. Pro-
20   fessio vero publica, in suis elementis constitu-
21   tivis coram Deo et Ecclesia considerata, melior
22   est cum ligamine perpetuo quam cum vinculo
23   temporaneo suscepta. Dispari enim illa firmita-
24   te diverso etiam gradu quis vivendi formam
25   Christi et Sanctae Ecclesiae, cum Sponso suo
26   indissolubiliter unitate, in oboedientia, pauper-
27   tate et sacra virginitate imitatur.

40 rentiam et oboedientiam secundum canonicas
41 leges praestare debent Episcopis, ob eorum in

1 Ecclesiis particularibus auctoritatem pastoralem
2 et ob necessariam in labore apostolico unita-
3 tem et concordiam (6).
4 *Ecclesia autem professionem religiosam*
5 *(C)non tantum sua sanctione ad status cano-*
6 *nici dignitatem erigit, sed eam ut statum Deo*
7 *consecratum etiam actione sua liturgica exhi-*
8 *bet. Ipsa enim Ecclesia, auctoritate sibi a Deo*
9 *commissa, profitentium vota suscipit, prece sua*
10 *publica eis auxilia et gratiam a Deo impetrat,*
11 *eos Deo commendat eisque spiritualem bene-*
12 *dictionem impertitur, oblationem eorum sacri-*
13 *ficio eucharistico adsocians.*
14 46. (olim n. 36, § § 1-2 et n. 35). *(Aesti-*
15 *manda est* consecratio per *consilia evangelica).*
16 *(A) Sollicite attendant religiosi (B),* ut per
17 ipsos Ecclesia revera Christum in dies, *sive*
18 *fidelibus sive infidelibus,* melius commonstret,
19 vel in monte contemplantem, vel turbis *Re-*
20 *gnum Dei annuntiantem,* vel aegrotos et sau-
21 cios sanantem ac peccatores ad bonam frugem
22 convertentem, vel pueris benedicentem, et om-
23 nibus benefacientem, *semper autem voluntati*
24 *Patris qui Eum misit oboedientem (7).*
25 Omnes tandem perspectum habeant (C),
26 consiliorum evangelicorum professionem,
27 quamvis renuntiationem secumferat bonorum

LATIN TEXT

28   Omnes tandem christifideles perspectum
29   habeant, consiliorum evangelicorum praxim,
30   quamvis renuntiationem secum ferat quorum-
31   dam bonorum certo laudabilium, vero profe-
32   ctui personae humanae tamen non obstare sed
33   summopere prodesse. Consilia enim, in carita-
34   te et secundum cuiusque personalem vocatio-
35   nem suscepta, ad affectuum humanorum puri-
36   ficationem et spiritualem libertatem non parum
37   conferunt, fervorem caritatis iugiter excitant,
38   variis modis humanae societati promovendae
39   prosunt, et praesertim ad vitae genus, quod
40   pro se elegit Christus Dominus, quodque Ma-
41   ter Eius virgo subsecuta est, hominem christia-
42   num magis conformant.

1
2
3
4
5
6
7
8   36. *(Conclusio).* Idcirco Sacra Synodus in
9   nomine Domini confirmat ac laudat innumeros
10   viros ac mulieres, Fratres ac Sorores, qui fideli
11   et humili praxi praedictae consecrationis Spon-
12   sam Christi condecorant omnibusque homini-
13   bus generosa atque diversissima servitia prae-
     stant.

28 quae indubie *magni aestimanda veniunt,* ta-
29 men personae humanae vero profectui non
30 obstare, sed *natura sua ei* summopere prodesse.
31 Consilia enim, secundum cuiusquam persona-
32 lem vocationem *voluntarie* suscepta, ad *cordis*
33 purificationem et spiritualem libertatem non
34 parum conferunt, fervorem caritatis iugiter ex-
35 citant et praesertim ad *genus vitae virginalis*
36 *ac pauperis,* quod sibi elegit Christus Domi-
37 nus, quodque Mater Eius Virgo amplexa est,
38 hominem christianum magis conformare *valent,*
39 ut exemplo tot sanctorum fundatorum compro-
40 batur. Nec quisquam aestimet religiosos con-
41 secratione sua aut ab hominibus alienos aut inu-
42 tiles in civitate terrestri fieri (D). Nam etsi

1 quandoque coaetaneis suis non directe adsi-
2 stunt, profundiore tamen modo eos in visceri-
3 bus Christi praesentes habent atque cum eis
4 spiritualiter cooperantur, ut aedificatio terre-
5 nae civitatis semper in Domino fundetur ad
6 Ipsumque dirigatur, ne forte in vanum labo-
7 raverint qui aedificant eam (8).
8   Idcirco denique Sacra Synodus confirmat
9 et laudat (E) viros ac mulieres, Fratres ac So-
10 rores, qui *in monasteriis, vel in scholis et noso-*
11 *comiis, vel in missionibus,* fideli et humili prae-
12 dictae consecrationis praxi Sponsam Christi
13 condecorant, omnibusque hominibus generosa
14 ac diversissima servitia praestant.

14	Meminerint ergo omnes peculiariter vocati,
15	suum esse commune in caritate officium ut per
16	ipsos Ecclesia revera Christum in dies melius
17	commonstret, vel in monte contemplantem,
18	vel ad turbas concionantem, vel aegrotos et
19	saucios sanantem ac peccatores ad bonam fru-
20	gem convertentem, vel pueris benedicentem,
21	vel denique omnibus benefacientem.
22	Quoniam vero omnes fideles ad sancitatem
23	spiritu evangelico prosequendam tenentur,
24	unusquisque sedulo curet, ut in qua vocatione
25	vocatus est, in ea permaneat atque magis excel-
26	lat, ad maiorem gloriam Christi, qui omnis
27	sanctitatis est origo et exemplar, et ad uberiorem
28	Ecclesiae sanctitatem.

---

15   47. (olim n. 36, § 3). *(Conclusio)*. (A)
16 Unusquisque ergo fidelis sedulo curet, ut in
17 quamcumque vocationem a Deo vocatus est,
18 in ea permaneat atque magis excellat, ad ube-
19 riorem Ecclesiae sanctitatem, ad maiorem glo-
20 riam unius et indivisae Trinitatis, quae in Chri-
21 sto et per Christum est omnis sanctitatis fons
22 et origo.

NOTAE

Caput VI (sive: cap. V, sectio B) - *De Religiosis*

Ad n. 43.

(1) Cf. ROSWEYDUS, *Vitae Patrum,* Antwerpiae, 1628. *Apophtegmata Patrum,* PG 65. PALLADIUS, *Historia Lausiaca:* PG 34, 991 ss.; ed. C. BUTLER, Cambridge 1898 (1904). PIUS XI, Const. Apost. *Umbratilem,* 8 iul. 1924: AAS 16 (1924) pp. 386-387. PIUS XII, Alloc. *Nous sommes heureux,* 11 apr. 1958: AAS 50 (1958) p. 283.

(2) Cf. *Cod. Iur. Can.,* c. 487 et 488 4°. PIUS XII, Alloc. *Annus sacer,* 8 dec. 1950: AAS 43 (1951) p. 27 s. PIUS XII, Const. Apost. *Provida Mater,* 2 febr. 1947: AAS 39 (1947) p. 120 ss.

Ad n. 44.

(3) Cf. S. THOMAS, *Summa Theol.* II-II, q. 184, a. 3 et q. 188, a. 2. S. BONAVENTURA, Opusc. XI, *Apologia Pauperum,* c. 3, 3: ed. Opera, Quaracchi, t. 8, 1898, p. 245 a.

Ad n. 45.

(4) Cf. CONC. VAT. I, Schema *De Ecclesia Christi,* cap. XV, et Adnot. 48: MANSI 51, 549 s. et 619 s. LEO XIII, Epist. *Au milieu des consolations,* 23 dec. 1900: ASS 33 (1900-01) p. 361. PIUS XII, Const. Apost. *Provida Mater,* 1. c. p. 114 s.

(5) Cf. LEO XIII, Const. *Romanos Pontifices,* 8 maii 1881: ASS 13 (1880-81) p. 483. PIUS XII, Alloc. *Annus sacer,* 8 dec. 1950: AAS 43 (1951) p. 28 s.

(6) Cf. PIUS XII, Alloc. *Annus sacer,* 1. c. p. 28. PIUS XII, Const. Apost. *Sedes Sapientiae,* 31 maii 1956: AAS 48 (1956) p. 355.

Ad n. 46.

(7) Cf. PIUS XII, Litt. Encycl. *Mystici Corporis,* 29 iun. 1943: AAS 35 (1943) p. 214 s.

(8) Cf. PIUS XII, Alloc. *Annus sacer,* 1. c. p. 30. Alloc. *Sous la maternelle protection,* 9 dec. 1957: AAS 50 (1958) p. 39 s.

Biography

Rev. Ralph M. Wiltgen, S.V.D., born December 17, 1921, in Chicago, was ordained a Divine Word priest in 1950 at Techny, Illinois, and obtained a doctorate in Missiology at the Pontifical Gregorian University in Rome in 1953. His first book, *Gold Coast* (now Ghana) *Mission History 1471-1880,* is sold out, and his history of Vatican II, *The Rhine Flows Into the Tiber: The Unkown Council,* is in its second printing. He founded and directed an independent six-language Council News Service which had more than 3000 subscribers in 108 countries. He is now writing and doing research for a three-volume history of the Catholic Church in New Guinea, and has been invited to write church histories for three other countries in Africa and Oceania. He has a reading knowledge of eight languages, speaks five of them, and on occasion serves as a simultaneous interpreter for international conferences. Since being assigned to Rome in 1960 he has published over 1500 pages of mission and church history and news in magazines, reviews, and news service bulletins. He has articles in the *New Catholic Encyclopedia* and has been invited to contribute four chapters to the monumental history of the Sacred Congregation for Evangelizing Peoples, now in preparation to mark that Congregation's 350th anniversary in 1972. He is listed in the *Pacific Islands Who's Who* and is a member of the "Société des Océanistes" of Paris. In the United State he has served as the national publicity director of the Divine Word Missionaries, and in Rome as their international publicity director. Currently he is residing in Rome.

INDEX

To Paragraph Numbers

in the Constitution on the Church